GW00579471

HALSALL

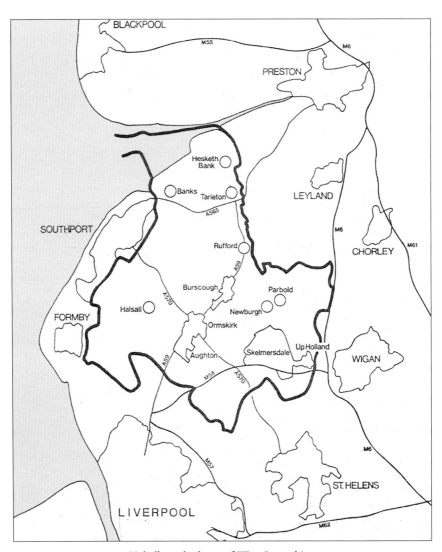

Halsall, at the heart of West Lancashire.

HALSALL

The village built on a rock

JOHN COTTERALL

Carnegie Publishing Ltd, 2000

Published by Carnegie Publishing Ltd
Carnegie House, Chatsworth Road
Lancaster LA1 4SL

First published December 2000

British Library Cataloguing-in-Publication data
A CIP record for this book is available from the British Library

ISBN 1–85936–082–3

Typeset in Adobe Garamond by Carnegie Publishing
Printed and bound in the UK by
The Cromwell Press, Trowbridge, Wilts

Contents

The Saracen's Head and Canal Bridge, Halsall, from an early twentieth-century postcard.

Foreword

THERE ARE A NUMBER of mysteries about Halsall – not least why such a large and fine church was built here at a time when there were very few people living in the area! Some unanswered questions, I suppose, will remain with their origins lost in the so-called 'Dark Ages'.

Since moving to Halsall, some six years ago, I have sought a history of the village in vain. Neighbouring Ormskirk and Birkdale, which have become larger places, have their histories, and my predecessor, the late Canon Bullough, produced a history of the present church. At last John Cotterall has put together a fascinating miscellany of Halsall – its history, its life – in one book. I, for one, and I am sure others who have a place in their hearts for the village, are very grateful to him. It answers some of the questions about Halsall, leaving others, as yet, still mysteries. Perhaps someone who enjoys this book, as I have done, will be encouraged to follow on and add to our knowledge and understanding. It would please John Cotterall if his work and enthusiasm were to lead to further insights into this place and its long history.

I commend this book to you – you should find it fascinating!

(Canon) Peter Goodrich,
Rector of Halsall, October 2000

About the Author

J OHN COTTERALL was born in Manchester but has lived in Southport since 1939. He started his working life in the Wigan Trustee Savings Bank where he met his wife. They now have three grown-up children and seven grandchildren. Serving as a naval officer during the war, he took a London University external degree and become a teacher. He then moved into educational administration with posts in Bolton, Salford, Chorley and Preston, where he retired as District Education Officer in 1989. He was one of the team of officers making the arrangements for the 1992 Preston Guild. His previous books have included *The West Lancashire Railway, North Meols to South Ribble, Preston's Palaces of Pleasure* (A history of the cinema in Preston) and *How Southport Got its Churches.* John is a lay reader at St John's Church, Birkdale.

All royalties from sales of this book are being donated to the Halsall White Heather and Sunshine Clubs.

CHAPTER ONE

A Lovely Village

Drive slowly and see our town – Drive quickly and see our jail! [2]

T HE FIRST THINGS you notice about Halsall are the traffic calming measures and, as you go through the village (observing the speed limit!), you see all that is expected of a typical Lancashire rural community – the church, a one-time pub alongside, the village stream, the school. The road is the A567 coming off the main Southport–Ormskirk road at the main gate to Scarisbrick Hall and eventually reaching Maghull via Lydiate. Sandwiched then between Scarisbrick and Lydiate, Halsall is, to the compilers of *The Treasures of Lancashire*,[2] a 'lovely village' lying 'within richly fertile farming land which has been won from the extensive Halsall Moss and is situated just over three miles to the north west of Ormskirk'. It 'extends from the pretty hamlets of Primrose Hill and Bangors Green on the outskirts of Ormskirk, west to the Southport boundary at Ainsdale, and has a population of about 1,920'.[3]

There are many questions that those interested in the history of West Lancashire will want to ask about Halsall. Why did the centre of the village develop where it has? What has been its history? What of folk who owned the land, and who worked on it? What of the church and the other historic buildings? How have travellers got to and from Halsall over the centuries? What are the memories of present-day villagers? Answers to these questions – and others that arise – will reveal a lot more than appears on the surface.

Perhaps it is impertinent for someone like me, not living in the village, to write about Halsall. But, over the years, I have become more and more interested in our part of Lancashire. Compared with other parts of the country, we are too modest about the wonderful historical heritage of which we are part. Those teachers who gave me my first enthusiasm for history were so busy trying to get me through public examinations that there was very little time to apply national developments to our local situation. If only they could have said, 'This is how the monasteries operated near where we are now living', or 'The Reformation worked out in Lancashire in this sort of way', or 'The Industrial Revolution was pioneered in

Lancashire in places very close to where we now live', or 'Here's a local example of Victorian Life!' This sort of approach would, I now realise, have brought history much more to life. We would not have been short, certainly in Halsall, of fascinating local examples of what was happening on a national scale. We can only hope that the national curriculum in our schools is now putting the matter right.

When I discovered that although there is a lot of published material about Halsall, nobody, with the exception of Canon Bullough,[4] has apparently done much recently to assemble it all in one place, I thought I would attempt to do that; at least on a modest scale writing as an enthusiast rather than a trained historian.

I could not have made any real progress without the help of Jim and Dorothy Sephton. Jim was brought up on Poplar Farm in Barton and Dorothy (a Carr before her marriage) lived at Gettern and Holt's farms in the Carr Moss Lane area where her father was farm manager. It is extremely sad that Dorothy died before being able to see the book in print. It has been Jim and Dorothy's unwritten knowledge of the area which has, I hope, enabled me to bring some of the history to life. I am extremely grateful to them. In the same context, I much appreciate the tremendous help given by Barry Critchley – his enthusiasm is infectious! Barry's wife Barbara has also been very supportive and encouraging. Councillor Margaret Edwards of Scarisbrick, Phil Coghlan of the *Southport Visiter* and Angela Birchall, former editor of the *Village Visiter*, have also been very co-operative. Mrs Margaret Evans of Aughton has made available to me the 1940s' picture of Halsall Football Club.

Thanks also to my valuable friends in the Southport Reference Library and to the obliging folk at Ormskirk Library, as well as those in the Lancashire Local History Library and the Lancashire Record Office in Preston. I also appreciate the help and encouragement of the Rector, Canon Peter Goodrich, who has written such a helpful Foreword.

John Hinchliffe, Conservation Officer for West Lancashire District Council, has also been very supportive with information and pictures, as has his colleague Alan Wright from the same office. Elaine Woodhead, Clerk to Halsall Parish Council, has gone to a great deal of trouble to make the Council's minutes available to me.

Pictures provided by Audrey Garlick, Jim Sephton, Graham Sutton, Andrew Cotterall, West Lancashire District Council are acknowledged with thanks. The response to Barry Critchley's request for photographs has been amazing – thank you to all who provided these photographs. The list of these folk includes: Mrs Annie Shacklady; Mrs Mary Hick; Mrs Winnie Lewis; Jim Heaton; Halsall CE Primary School; Bill Neale; Dick and Nancy

Ainscough; Miss Margaret Howard; Ron and Jeanne Burgess; and Mrs Betty Balmer.

I am grateful to Carnegie Publishing for having enough confidence in me to publish the book. With some other Carnegie publications I have been the 'gofer'; it's nice, at last, to have your own show! My thanks also to my wife and family for putting up with my excursions into local history and assisting with proof reading. I have mentioned other help in footnotes and I am indebted to everyone who helped in what has been, at least for me, a very satisfying venture.

John Cotterall,
October 2000.

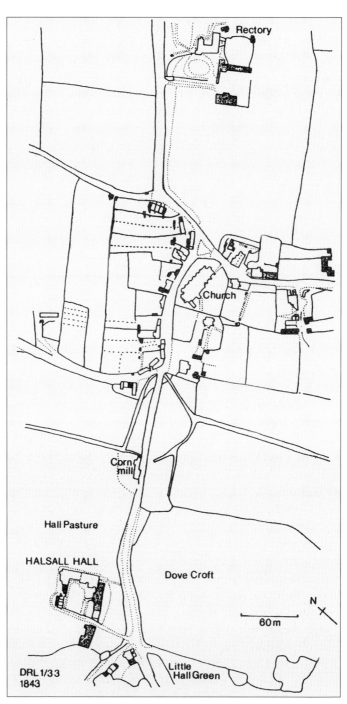

An 1843 map of the village.

CHAPTER TWO

Water, Water Everywhere . . .

Water, water, everywhere
Nor any drop to drink[1]

W EST LANCASHIRE's bore holes are a valuable resource. There is no shortage of drinking water. At one time, however, there was a lot more water – too much in fact – above the surface. It was mainly concentrated in three lakes – White Otter (in the present-day Mill Lane area of Ainsdale), Black Otter (a mile to the south) and Gettern Mere (half a mile to the south-east).

Halsall village, therefore, originally grew up on rock. Experience showed that, in the days before piling and 'rafts', the moss was not suitable for development. Unlike some local areas, folk followed the scriptural advice that it was the wise rather than the foolish man who built his house on the rock! The drainage of Martin Mere, in neighbouring Scarisbrick, resulted in much public recognition of those involved. 'A man truly ingenious, urbane and pleasant', says the Latin plaque in St Cuthbert's, Churchtown, about Thomas Fleetwood who obtained an Act of Parliament in 1692 to drain the Mere. Thomas Eccleston – one of the Scarisbricks – received a Gold Medal from The Society for the Encouragement of the Arts, Manufacture and Commerce for the professional drainage work he commissioned a hundred years later.

In contrast, the draining of the less stable parts of the Halsall area was much more low-key. Dr Alan Crosby[2] reminds us that 'in no part of West Lancashire (and indeed in virtually no part of England) is the landscape we see today truly 'natural' – almost invariably it is the product of man's influence'. 'Drainage in the area between Halsall and Altcar [continues Dr Crosby] was already in progress in the thirteenth century, particularly by the monks of Burscough and of Merevale Abbey (Warwickshire) both of which monasteries had extensive estates here.' The draining – slower and more piecemeal than in some other areas – was completed by 1750.

Sylvia Harrop[3] pays particular tribute to Edward Segar of Barton House, Barton south of Halsall. A near relation to the Halsall family, he inherited mosslands which he began to reclaim in the early 1700s. The land in question was divided into 2-acre fields surrounded by 5-foot ditches. These were cleaned out after a year and, a year later, the ground was firm enough to take men and horses. The following winter, the top surface was removed and burned and then ploughed with a horse which was shod, duck-like, with 18-inch wide oval boards to prevent it sinking into the peat. The turf that was ploughed was burned and there was a second ploughing and burning the following August with the resulting hot ashes ploughed into the soil. Rye was sown in September and, after this, two crops of rye or oats were sown with the land then being in grass for three or four years.

It was a costly and lengthy process lasting seven or eight years, but the end product was well worth-while and provided well-placed areas of very good arable land to feed the populations in towns like Liverpool, which were growing as a result of the Industrial Revolution. It was in the middle of this area of mossland that the village of Halsall grew and developed. The main concentration of buildings stood, says W. T. Bulpit,[4] 'on an outcrop of the New Sandstone. This series of rock contains salt, and the name Halsall implies salt'. When Bulpit wrote in 1908, the curfew still rang out from the church in the winter months to 'guide the belated traveller' over what was – and still is in some areas – a very lonely and remote part of West Lancashire.

'Judging by the situation of the various villages and hamlets,' says the *Victoria History of the County of Lancashire*,[5] 'it may be asserted that, in this part of West Lancashire, the 25-feet level formed the boundary of the habitable district in ancient times. All below it was swamp, which formed a broad and definite division between Halsall Parish on the east and Formby and Ainsdale on the west.'

The same authority suggests a 'line drawn southward from Halsall village to pass a quarter of a mile or so to the eastward of the villages of Lydiate and Maghull'. To the west of this line, the rock formation consists of lower keuper sandstone – defined as a common sort of rock consisting of sand grains consolidated with materials such as quartz, haematite and clay. Bearing in mind that the coastline was once significantly eastward of its present position, we can expect to find rock of this nature. Nor, when we look at some of the buildings in the parish, are we surprised to see that this sort of sandstone is widely used in building.

To the north west of a line drawn from the site of the former Barton/ Halsall Station on Carr Moss Lane to Scarisbrick Bridge on the canal, keuper marl occurs. 'Carr' is ancient Norse and refers, significantly, to an area of bog or fen in which scrub, especially willow, has become established.[6] 'Keuper', the reference book tells us,[7] means that the rock formation

developed during the Triassic Period of rock formation, and that we are dealing with developments which took place 184 to 195 million years ago!

Halsall has been described as a 'miasmatic district' [8] – a phrase meaning 'an unwholesome or foreboding atmosphere – pollution in the atmosphere especially noxious vapours from decomposing organic matter'.[9] The situation reminds 'one of the similar situation of the famous Isle of Avalon', says C. W. Budden.[10] There have long been suggestions that King Arthur trod the banks of the River Douglas but any suggestion that Halsall was part of the equation is perhaps a new idea!

The name 'Halsall' comes from the Domesday name *Heleshale*, meaning 'rising ground near the edge of the great bog or moss' [11] – a moss stretching out to the coast – in this case a distance of four-and-a-half miles. At one stage a forested area, tree trunks are still regularly dug up. Refreshing and lively breezes invariably blow in from the Irish Sea.

A general impression of the whole area can be gained from a document issued by the West Lancashire District Council.[12] Combining the areas of Scarisbrick, Halsall and Haskayne, the document lists the following characteristics:

1. Low, undulating land rising to the Clieves Hills prominently visible from mosslands to the west. Panoramic views to the south west and north from the higher ground. [The most prominent building on the Clieves Hills is Christ Church, Aughton on the Ormskirk/Liverpool road.]

2. Farmland, mainly intensive arable.

3. Little woodland.

4. Trees relatively scarce, associated with settlements and houses and farmsteads – some in hedgerows.

5. Large irregular-shaped fields.

6. Minor channels and ditches as field boundaries.

7. Few hedges usually frequently cut – some associated with banks.

8. Main roads meandering with numerous meandering minor roads.

9. Many farmsteads and settlements round a central building.

The village of Halsall and the causeway and the few remains of the mill and sluice are highlighted as being of particular County Landscape Importance. The Leeds and Liverpool Canal is important for industrial archaeology. We must, says the document, 'enhance wildlife habitats within the canal and in adjacent areas. Avoid potentially polluting developments. Avoid developments which will significantly disturb wildlife'.

The *Victoria County History* [13] gives a summary of the produce of the area in 1907. Corn, root crops, fodder and hay are listed. Some pasture land exists, and the entry 'Occasional osier beds fill up odd corners' suggests some trade, as in nearby Mawdesley, in basket-making (baskets of all sorts were very important before the days of modern packaging). The soil is referred to as loamy with clay underneath, and reference is made to flooding in wet weather: 'Deep ditches are necessary to carry away superfluous water'. The 'natural recepticle of all the streams and ditches' is the River Alt. The same ditches, in summer, being 'filled with a luxuriant fenland flora which thus finds shelter in an exposed country'. The absence of trees is put down to west winds laden with salt. 'The ground rises gently to the east; until the boundary 95 feet is reached'. 'A natural curiosity of the district', says the history, 'is the bituminous turf, formerly used for lighting instead of candles.'

No less a proportion than 72 per cent of the land in West Lancashire is agricultural land graded 1 or 2. In Lancashire as a whole the percentage is only 14 per cent, while nationally the figure is 18 er cent.[14] Drainage of difficult areas has enabled Halsall to contribute very effectively to the

Above: John Ball at work on Gregory Farm during the war years.

Below: A wonderful photograph of traditional ploughing. Unfortunately we have not (yet) been able to identify the ploughman.

Few photographs illustrate better a typical West Lancashire landscape of two generations ago. An unidentified farmer or farm worker (perhaps one of the Ball family) and his team stand amid seemingly endless and featureless, yet highly fertile, fields.

significant percentage which West Lancashire can boast. A former resident of a Halsall farm [15] – born there in 1914 – gives an interesting picture of agriculture in his younger days. The main concentration was on cash crops. Land, not on the moss, was usually cultivated on a four-year rotation as follows:

Year 1. Sown twice for hay, mown in June – a smaller crop in September. Deep ploughing in the winter.

Year 2. April – early potatoes planted. Late May/early June – a ridging plough would earth them up. A 'rucker' would then loosen the soil in the bottom of the drill and make 'rucks' – small heaps 20 inches apart. Cabbages – usually savoy – would be hand-planted on these ricks between rows of potatoes. In later years, cauliflowers replaced cabbages. In June, a special fork was used to dig out the potatoes, the tops of which were placed between the cabbages where they rotted away leaving a field of cabbage behind. The savoys were marketed in winter.

Year 3. In March, oats were sown and harvested in the autumn. Wheat was then sown in October/November.

A youthful Charlie Carr is sitting on the planter; James Cheetham is holding the horse.

Year 4. The wheat was harvested in the spring and the land was harrowed and sown with grass and clover mixture to provide the following year's [year 1's] hay crop.

Jim Sephton explains further:

The grass and clover seeds were sown in the spring – a system known as 'underscoring' – the wheat being, at that time, 3 " to 6 " high. The wheat was harrowed twice – once before and once after sowing. It was then rolled. After the wheat was cut in August, the field was then referred to as 'clover root'.

Some fields were devoted to spring cabbage sown in late July, transplanted in September, growing during the winter and marketed April onwards. Land on the mosslands, subject to flooding, was farmed quite differently. There was no winter crop. Oats were grown and alternated with main crop potatoes. There were occasional fields of celery, hay and cabbage.

The cultivation of potatoes is, of course, particularly linked with West Lancashire. Those of us educated locally were taught that we lived in the Ormskirk potato-growing district of Lancashire – an area which, along

Mechanisation, when it came to Halsall, progressed speedily after the war. Tom or John Ball sits proudly on a Fordson. Note the facility on the rear wheels to add a second set of tyres, essential for wetter times of the year.

with areas like south-west Scotland, Lincolnshire, Cornwall and Ireland, is very involved in this type of agriculture. Significantly, perhaps, an Irish ship, said to have been wrecked off Marshside north of Southport in 1565, was carrying the first potatoes imported into Britain. [16] This area could well have pioneered English potato growing. Ulster Prince and Ulster Sceptre were the preferred species until the 1980s but they have now been superseded by better yielding varieties such as Dundrod and Maris Bard. Whether or not they taste as good as earlier varieties is open to question! [17] By the mid-eighteenth century, potatoes rivalled bread as the main food for feeding the growing numbers of working people in the new towns.

Until the Second World War, although larger farms could afford tractors, most farmers resisted change and heavy work continued to be done by horses. In Barton alone (according to Jim Sephton) there were 30 to 40 horses and considerably more in the township of Halsall.

Traditional farming philosophy was 'waste not, want not'. Livestock was usually a sideline or, in many cases, a means of providing food for the family. Every farm had its cow for milk and butter. Pigs, reared on household scraps, hay, straw, corn and waste potatoes, provided bacon and ham, salted down in winter, for use throughout the year. Free-range poultry produced eggs and there was a bird for the table as required. The sale of eggs surplus to requirements gave the farmer's wife a little pocket money! Every farm had its orchard, providing fruit such as pears, apples, plums, damsons, currants, gooseberries and rhubarb. Kitchen gardens yielded a good supply of vegetables. In the days when Halsall was part of the Scarisbrick Estate, everything – timber, bricks, drainage tiles and items for repairs – came from the estate yard at the Hall. Workmen came out to do the work.

The horse-drawn fire engine *c.*1880 in the Botanic Gardens Museum used by volunteer crews from Scarisbrick, Halsall and Haskayne is a reminder that provision was also made for emergencies. Several teams of volunteers were required to work the pump levers to raise water. There were only relatively small sets of ladders and the in-built toolbox carried standpipes, hydrant keys, branch pipes, wrenches etc.[18]

John Cropper, who farmed two hundred acres based on Halsall Hall, was perhaps the exception in not wanting to concentrate on cash crops. Speaking in 1973,[19] he said, 'I still think that, even in these days of streamlined systems, land is always better for having cattle on it'. At that time, he had 50 head of black and whites, buying animals 15–18 months old and passing them on two years later to Wigan and Preston markets. The livestock on this particular farm were fed on the residue available from vegetable growing.

With the demise of local shops and the advent of supermarkets and trade with Europe, Halsall, like most Lancashire villages, has difficulties with the large vehicles sent to collect produce from bigger farm units; three-ton trailers have been replaced by twelve-ton vehicles. Road safety problems have arisen and units of this sort going on to mosslands can crush drains which are near the surface.[20] Any county get-together of parish council representatives confirms that Halsall is not alone in noticing these changes.

CHAPTER THREE

God Bless the Squire[1]

The rich man in his castle,
The poor man at his gate,
God made them high and lowly,
And ordered their estate.[2]

AFTER THE CONQUEST, William the Conqueror distributed land in various parts of the country to those who had assisted him in his invasion. In 1066, Chetel – presumably a Saxon – held what was a principal manor in the district. It is granted to the Lord of Warrington, who must have pleased William. Then the French names appear. Pain de Vilers gives Halsall to Vivian Gernet when he marries his daughter Emma. In 1212, Robert de Vilers is Lord of Halsall. 'Desiring prayers only in return', the family gave some lands in Halsall, including pasture at Renacres, to the Premonstratensian Abbey at Cockersands near Cockerham. As the abbey had only been founded in 1190, this gift must have been useful to the monks.[3]

All this is an interesting example of the Norman maxim:

The knight fought,
The peasant worked,
The monk prayed.

Often, as payment for these prayers, it was marginal land, not profitable for normal cultivation, that was given. At this time, Halsall would not have been short of such land and, as we have seen, it often fell to monks to initiate drainage schemes in the late medieval period.

In 1212, Alan, son of Simon, holds the land for Robert de Vilers. The first Halsall to be mentioned is Alan de Halsall, otherwise called 'de Lydiate'. This is the beginning of the Halsall association with the estate which lasted right up to 1625. Alan is thought to have been the husband of a Gernet heiress – Alice. He is succeeded by his son Simon who granted some land to the Prior and Canons of Burscough. The church links are now getting nearer home.

In the 1300s, we have matrimonial problems. In 1325, Gilbert de Halsall 'made an agreement with Henry de Atherton as to the marriage of his son Oates with Henry's sister Margaret and settled upon his son, and his wife, lands in Halsall and Barton'. Oates succeeds his father in 1346 and, we are told, 'the marriage arranged for him in infancy did not prove altogether satisfactory'. Oates 'unlawfully allied himself with Katherine de Coudray' and the aggrieved Margaret had to refer her case to the Bishop of Lichfield – in whose patch Halsall was situated – to get maintenance. This adultery had The Black Death as its backdrop. Richard Ball Howard[4] identifies Kathleen de Coudray as being one of only two members of the de Coudray family who survived the plague. She was married to Richard de Aghton (sic) whose family came to North Meols because of the plague.

Gilbert de Halsall, made a knight in 1388, fought in the French Wars. Henry became a parson and was made Rector by Sir Gilbert in 1395, becoming Archdeacon of Chester twenty years later. Richard de Halsall had been Rector from 1336 to 1365 but Henry de Halsall's will (he died in 1522) put the whole arrangement about having a member of the ruling family as parson on a much firmer basis. If at all possible, the living should now go to a family member; if a vacancy occurred while a likely candidate was still under age, the trustees must present 'one of the next of his blood'. Failing this, some person of good conversation whom the trustees might judge would be 'loving and kind to his heirs' should be chosen. Attitude to parishioners did not seem to enter into the equation! Land was set aside with a yearly value of £4 6s. 8d. to find 'an honest and well-disposed priest' to pray and do divine service in Halsall Church for ever for his soul [Henry] and that of his deceased wife Margaret'.

In the protestant era of Elizabeth I, Edward Halsall is described as 'conformable but otherwise of no good note'. In his will he asked to be buried in the church or chancel of Halsall – a reminder of the subtle distinction between the parts of the building housing the altar (for the clergy) and the nave (for the ecclesiastically 'rank and file'). The wording Edward used is rather quaint: 'Wishing (although it may seem but vanity) that such parts of Ursula, my late wife, and of Richard my son as shall then remain unconsumed may be taken out of the Parish Church of Prescot where they were buried and laid in the grave with me, where also I am very desirous to have Anne now my wife (when God shall call her) likewise to lie, if it may so stand with God's pleasure, to the end that we may altogether joyfully rise at the last day, to live (as my hope it is we shall) with Christ our Lord everlasting in His Glorious Kingdom.'

The phrase 'otherwise of no good note', describing Edward, is explained when we see from his will that he says, 'I trust to die a member of God's

Catholic Church'. Even though, on the surface, he conformed to Elizabeth's requirements, at heart he still adhered to the 'Old Faith'. He was, like so many, a secret recusant.

His successor was 21-year-old Cuthbert, illegitimate son of Henry Halsall (of Halsall Grammar School fame). His early career was successful – he was a JP by the age of twenty-two! Knighted in 1599, Cuthbert was certainly in the 'Old Faith' category, but he was more openly a rebel and suffered financially. His later antics have given him the label 'The Bad Sir Cuthbert'.

Perhaps his troubles started with his marriage to Dorothy, illegitimate daughter of the 4th Earl of Derby. As one of the richest and most powerful families in Lancashire, the Derbys enjoyed a lavish lifestyle which Cuthbert sought to emulate. He was also very much associated with the Earl of Essex, which did not, apparently, help the situation. Because of mounting debts Cuthbert began selling land in 1618. In 1617, he mortgaged Renacres for £1,000 and Sir Charles Gerard bought Halsall and Downholland in 1625. Robert Blundell bought Birkdale, Meandale ('then part of Birkdale and now lost', says Sylvia Harrop) and Ainsdale in 1632. By 1631 Cuthbert was in a debtors' prison and Halsall had to be sold to his grandson Sir Charles Gerard – Master of the Rolls to Queen Elizabeth and thereafter, presumably, a conformist. He died about 1640 in York and is buried in Halsall, where he is particularly remembered because he actually resided in the hall – something rather unusual! He built a windmill and water mill in the parish and continued long-running disputes with Robert Blundell of Ince about boundaries with Birkdale, Ainsdale and Renacres. Three of his sons fought for the King in the Civil War.

Charles – the eldest and the heir – was born in 1616 and distinguished himself sufficiently to become Baron Gerard of Brandon in the north-west corner of Suffolk near the Norfolk border. His commitment to the King forced him to quit the country during the Protectorate and he spent his exile planning to kill Cromwell. This earned various promotions at the Restoration. In 1678 he became Viscount Brandon and Earl of Macclesfield. Another period of exile followed because of his liaison with the Duke of Monmouth, who was an unsuccessful claimant to the English throne during the reign of James II. But Brandon returned with William of Orange to receive a further reward. Following his death in 1693, he was buried in Westminster Abbey. Although his involvement with Halsall may not have been very great, like his forebears, he managed to continue boundary disputes with the coastal areas.

His son Charles, born in Paris in 1659, was a knight of the shire and thus another Lord Brandon. He was convicted of high treason for his part in the Rye House Plot when, in 1693, a group of Whig extremists conspired to murder Charles II for his Roman Catholic leanings which, it was feared, would affect the succession. The plan was to murder the King and to proclaim the Duke of Monmouth – with whom his father had been involved – as king. The plot was foiled by an unexpected change in the King's plans. Some participants fled, others were executed. Charles was pardoned.

'It will not be easily forgotten', says the Kenyon MSS,[5] 'that Lord Brandon had two pardons – one for murder and another for high treason'. Surprisingly, after having been forgiven by the King, he became deputy lieutenant to Lord Molyneux, 'a grand papist' – a bit odd for someone once plotting to prevent a catholic succession! 'His actings may administer suspicion what his designs are,' says the manuscript. Questions are also raised about the unofficial storage of arms in Halsall and Liverpool Castle.

Charles died without legitimate issue in 1701 and was succeeded by his brother Fitton, who died a year later, also without issue. The two sisters, Elizabeth and Charlotte – joint heirs – brought problems because of the ultimate marriages of their respective daughters. Elizabeth died in 1700 and her share of the estate passed to her daughter – another Elizabeth who married James, Duke of Hamilton. Charlotte, when she died, left her share to her daughter, another Charlotte who married Lord Mohun. A dispute about ownership then arose and, in true eighteenth-century style, Hamilton and Mohun decided to fight it out in a duel staged on 15 November 1712 in Hyde Park. Sadly, both contestants were killed and the estate passed to Elizabeth Lawrence – second wife of Lord Mohun.

In *Vernacular Buildings on the Lancashire Plain* (N.W. Archaeological Trust, Report No. 2, 1987), Jennifer Lewis takes up the story: 'One of the widows, probably Elizabeth Lady Hamilton, took for her third husband Col Charles Mordaunt, son of General Lewis Mordaunt and nephew of the third Earl of Peterborough. There were no children from this marriage and the Gerard estates, including Halsall, passed to Mordaunt's heir, a son by his second marriage, Charles Mordaunt'.

And what a mark Mordaunt made on the estate! He had left the army in 1765 and was the first owner to live in the Hall for a century. His initials on rainwater heads on the building suggest that he made significant structural improvements. He was sufficiently astute to realise the potential of the Industrial Revolution and, in 1779, established a cotton mill in Halsall. Like others, he was threatened by pre-Luddite mobs and, in the year he established the mill, he wrote to the Secretary of War alerting him to the rioting mob in the parish. Fourteen soldiers and a sergeant were duly sent from Liverpool.

By 1781 the business was thriving, with 600 spindles and employment

Halsall Hall.

Above: The cellars at Halsall Hall, which were apparently used during the Industrial Revolution for tanning.

Below: As a working farm house, occupied by Cllr John Cropper.

for 160 poor women and children. There was probably both spinning and weaving on the site and the cellars of Halsall Hall had water tanks for textile manufacture and tanning. John Moon, superintendent of the works, negotiated with the pioneering firm of Boulton & Watt of Soho, Birmingham, for a steam engine to supplement the power supplied from the 18" waterwheel over which the water passed to power the original machines. The Hall seems to have been adapted after 1765 as housing accommodation for mill employees. The local minting, between 1783 and 1791, of Halsall 'pennies' as wages, suggests that Mordaunt may have operated a 'truck' system. Special tokens of this sort were only exchangeable in shops operated by the employer – arrangements which were eventually declared illegal in 1831.

Facing possible attacks from machine wreckers on the one hand, Mordaunt also faced the wrath of Industrial Revolution champion Richard Arkwright on the other, who commenced proceedings for an infringement of patents for carding, roving and drawing machines. Fortunately, an association of Lancashire spinners had anticipated the onslaught and Arkwright's legal arguments fell on deaf ears. His 'patents which held back his rivals, and thus the overall progress of the industry, were overturned in 1785', says David Hunt.[6] 'It was a popular verdict,' says Gordon Read,[7] 'in accordance with the British hatred of monopoly. The general opinion was that he had already received sufficient, in the fortune he had made, for his efforts.'

Although Mordaunt was in quite a different league from Arkwright, the continuing circulation of 'Halsall pennies' until at least 1791 suggests, in the words of Jennifer Lewis,[8] that 'Charles Mordaunt was involved in cotton manufacture in no small way'. The suggestion that there is a line of clay in the area of The Runnell, on the field to the right, and a hole that might have developed because clay was dug, may be a reminder that Mordaunt or some other enterprising landowners might have had other industrial ideas as well as cotton manufacture – brick-making was widespread in parts of West Lancashire.

Local resident Barry Critchley has provided the following information about Charles Mordaunt: 'Charles Lewis Mordaunt's initials and the date 1769 can be seen on a lead spout of the Hall which he reconstructed to make it a fashionable house. He put in a venetian window on a new west wing and built a great entertaining room with bedrooms above. He wrote for farming and other newspapers and tried to improve the agriculture in Halsall. He even built a spinning factory on the side of the stream below the house to use water power. The cattle pound for the village was just inside the main gate. There was a big garden but this was taken away when the causeway (the present main road) was built so that the ford across the brook could be disused.' Even though it would have needed a crane to move it, the great carved stone fireplace from the large west room was stolen some years ago.

Mordaunt died in his Ormskirk house, where he spent the winters, in 1808 at the age of 78. His successors do not seem to have continued the business. Had they done so, the history of the country area of Halsall might have been very different!

The folk taking over were, in fact, the Scarisbricks in the person of Thomas Eccleston. His interests, as we have noted, were primarily in industry. After Eccleston, came Charles Scarisbrick – 'the richest commoner in England' – who died in 1860 when his sister Lady Anne made a triumphant return to Scarisbrick Hall. On her death Halsall passed to her daughter, Eliza Margaret, who had married the French Count de Casteja who, in turn, inherited the property when his wife died. The Count was well thought of and it was said that he: 'made himself deservedly popular by his agreeable manners, and it was felt by all that they could not be wrong in looking forward to the son walking in the footsteps of a father known for his justice as a landlord and his kindness as a friend.' [9]

In 1890 the Castejas, along with Lord Derby, the Earl of Sefton and the Weld-Blundells, formed the quartet of West Lancashire's four great estates. With the break-up of the Halsall estate, most changes of landlord seem to have gone through without much comment; tenants, no doubt, realised that there was little they could do anyway. But more fundamental changes were on the way.

A local resident takes up the story: 'They [the Castejas] had a son, who became known as the Young Marquis and, about 1920, the farmers of the estate were invited to a dinner, after which they had a shock. The Marquis told them that he was selling the estate. The tenants had first option to buy their farms for 20 years' rent and several who had no mossland did this.' [10]

On 12 February 1921, *The Southport Visiter* [11] published a statement which aimed to clarify the situation. It confirmed that in the previous September, a syndicate of men associated with the commerce of Liverpool had purchased the estates. 170 farms had been involved. Tenants had the option of purchasing, at reasonable prices, the land they occupied and there was even a scheme of easy payments. Four thousand acres were recognised as being inferior to other areas of the estates in respect of ditching and drainage, but these problems would receive attention.

This (said the statement) was one of the oldest estates in the country belonging to the same family without being sold off into small holdings.

This was the first time land in the area had been offered for sale outside the family. Many tenants had bought their holdings but the right was reserved to sell it to outsiders. There had already been many outside offers to purchase.

Land remaining unsold was, in the event, sold to a Mr W. A. Towler of Littleport, Cambridge. The date was 30 August 1920. When the new owner invited the remaining local tenants to the Scarisbrick Arms for a series of three evening 'get-togethers' to talk about selling the land in small parcels, he met with an almost total boycott. A careful watch was kept on the pub to see exactly who was brave enough to accept the invitation to talk about the sale.[12]

Eventually, 'local gentlemen' opened negotiations for purchasing the land. A syndicate called The Scarisbrick, Halsall and Downholland Estate Limited was headed by Burscough potato merchant James Martland. Later the land was split up between various members of the group. The southern part went to a partner called Steel from Aughton.

But 'Marie Andre Leon Alvar de Biaudos Marquis de Casteja, DSO, MC.' (as the publicity describes him)[13] kept some interest in the estate despite the earlier sale. But on 9 August 1923, at The Drill Hall, Ormskirk, he instructed Messrs Boult, Son & Marples to auction 'The Outlying Portions of the Scarisbrick Hall Estate'. A number of Halsall properties were included and the sales literature enables us to identify the 1920s owners of the property, who had obviously taken the opportunity earlier of buying their holdings. The sale was well attended and there was 'spirited bidding' for some of the smaller properties. Several larger farms were withdrawn because of the reserve prices set.

The auctioneer stressed the depressed condition of agriculture. Experiences in West Lancashire were obviously similar to what was happening elsewhere. British agriculture had done well during the First World War, with the need for the country to grow its own food. Farmers had been guaranteed against loss. But peace brought lean times. Farmers were left unprotected against foreign competition at a time when world prices had fallen. Farm workers lost the protection of a minimum wage and many took better-paid jobs in the towns, where living conditions were often better. At the same time, the post-war period saw swift changes in agricultural methods. In 1914, there were hardly any motor tractors on British farms; by 1939, there were 50,000.

But despite the problems, the number of owner-occupiers in the country-side had increased significantly. War taxation and death duties led to the selling of estates such as Scarisbrick to sitting tenants who had been able to build up capital during the war years. Ex-servicemen had gratuities to invest. After 1930 these folk were able to benefit from considerably increased state aid.[14]

Some of those highlighted as being at the 1923 sale still have local connections in the area. They were: Messrs R. R. Glover; E. L. Biddlecombe; G. A. Brighouse; W. Kennedy; J. E. Hindle (Southport); A. Warde; C. S. Ellis; E. V. Taylor; G. Wilson (Southport). In addition there was a 'large sprinkling of local farmers and others interested in agriculture'.

At the sale, ground rents, with freeholds, were on offer relating to the following:

LOT 20 – Four cottages and land on the north side of Morris Lane with a frontage on to the canal near Weavers Bridge. The property was held on lease of Mr J. Draper of Railway Road, Ormskirk and the tenants of the cottages were: Mr William Sutton, Mr William Deacon, Mr John Parkes, Mr Robert Porter.
The ground rent was £1 8s. (£1.40) per annum but the item was withdrawn from the sale.

LOT 21 – Shop, House and Outbuildings on the south-west side of Halsall Lane fronting the canal and adjoining Halsall Warehouse Bridge. The lease was held by Mr E. Segar of Aughton and the occupant was Mr Edward Gore. The ground rent was £2 10s. (£2.50) but the item was withdrawn.

LOT 23 – Two cottages and land called 'Peet's Cottages' on the north-east side of New Cut Lane. John Ball had the lease and he and Hugh Cookson lived in the property. The ground rent of £3 per annum was sold to John Ball for £350 after 'spirited bidding'.

LOT 24 – Ground rent of £7 on land and four houses – Wood Vale Farm, Wood Vale Cottage, The Beeches and The Laurels near Woodvale Siding off Liverpool Road Birkdale, but described as Halsall. The lease was held by Mrs M. A. & S. A. Wheelwright who lived at the farm although the occupier is shown as Mr James Wheelwright. George Lancaster lived at the cottage, Miss Hastings at The Beeches and Samuel Gartside, who bought the ground rent for £135, at The Laurels.

LOT 26 – Semi-detached bungalow and land at the corner of Holt Lane and Ambrose Lane near New Ollery Hall. Joseph Kershaw and Thomas Rimmer lived there and the gound rent was £1 10s. (£1.50) per annum and it was sold privately.

LOT 27 – Two cottages and land called Moss Villas on the north side of Gregory lane. The occupants were Richard Fairclough and Richard Longton and the ground rent £4 per annum. This was sold for £1,320 to James and John Aspinall of White Otter Farm, Southport.

LOT 28 – Building Land on the north side of Segar's Lane opposite White

By Order of MARQUIS DE CASTEJA, D.S.O., M.C.

TO BE SOLD BY AUCTION

(UNLESS PREVIOUSLY DISPOSED OF BY PRIVATE TREATY)

BY MESSRS.

BOULT, SON & MAPLES

On THURSDAY, the 9th day of AUGUST, 1923

COMMENCING AT 2-30 O'CLOCK, AT

THE DRILL HALL
ORMSKIRK.

The Outlying Portions of the

"Scarisbrick Hall Estate"

INCLUDING

Eight Fully=Licensed Public Houses, Ground Rents,

Dwelling Houses, Cottages, Farms, Land,

Freehold Reversions, Detached Villa, etc.

SITUATE IN THE PARISHES OF

Scarisbrick, Halsall and Downholland

NEAR SOUTHPORT AND ORMSKIRK RESPECTIVELY

IN THE COUNTY OF LANCASTER.

For further Particulars, Plans, etc., apply to :—

The Auctioneers :	OR	The Solicitors :
BOULT, SON & MAPLES,		WELD & WELD,
Valuers and Estate Agents		15, Lord Street,
5, Cook Street,		Liverpool.
Liverpool.		

The Central Stationery & Printing Co. Ltd., 10, North John Street, Liverpool.

A poster advertising the sale of the estate, 9 August 1923.

Otter Farm.

Interestingly, the lease was held by the Mayor of Southport and the ground rent was £80 per annum.

LOT 29 – Farm buildings, three cottages and land known as Model Farm on the north and south sides of Plex Moss Lane. The lease was held by John Rimmer of Plex Moss Lane. The ground rent was £500 per annum and its sale was withdrawn at £7,590.

LOT 30 – Semi-detached bungalows and land on the south-west side of Renacres Lane adjoining Shirdley Hill Station. The lease was held by Mrs Mary Blundell of Renacres Lane and the tenants were Miss Dawson and Mrs Scarisbrick. The ground rent was £1 12s. (£1.60).

LOT 31 – A piece of land with a bungalow called Fern Lea on the south-west side of Renacres Lane near Shirdley Hill Station. The lease was again held by Mrs Mary Blundell and the tenants were John Sumner and William Rutledge. The ground rent of £2 per annum was sold to Mr Langford for £40.

Property actually for sale included:

LOT 33 – A bungalow called Fair View with land on the south-west side of Renacres Lane near the station. Mr Peter Tasker was the occupier and lease-holder and the ground rent of £4 3s. (£4.15) was sold for £76 to Annie Marshall of Shirdley Hill.

LOT 34 – Semi-detached cottages with land on the south side of New Cut Lane occupied by Mr R. Sharrocks, Mr Morris Reany and others. Mr S. Warde bought the ground rent of £21 per annum for £335.

Other ground rent sales included:

LOT 35 – Land and semi-detached bungalows on the south-west side of Renacres Lane near the station. The occupiers were Mr W. Sephton and Mr Peter Winnard and the ground rent was £3 10s. (£3.50) It was sold privately for £70.

LOT 36 – Two cottages and land on the west side of Renacres Lane near the station. Occupiers: Mr William Lea and Mr Peter Rimmer – ground rent £4 per annum. Mr W. Rimmer of Shirdley Hill bought it.

LOT 43 – Land and a pair of semi-detached houses called Brook Villas on the south side of Halsall Road. Mr John Sharrock of Boundary Farm, Halsall Road, Birkdale held the lease and George Sharrock and Mr Hulme lived in the houses. The ground rent was £10 per annum and was sold privately for £100.

LOT 49 – Rose Farm (17 acres) on the east and west sides of Halsall Road (or New Street). The tenant was Thomas Blundell. His ground rent was £49

During renovation work.

per annum and the tithe rent £6 3s. (£6.15) per annum. The tenure was already freehold and the sale of the ground rent was withdrawn at £1,055.

LOT 50 – Mill House Farm (79 acres) on the west side of Halsall Road (or New Street). The 79-acre site included a 5-bedroom house, stabling for 7 horses, a shippon for 8 cows, 2 pigsties, a garage and an ejector closet. The reference to an 'Irishman's House' is a reminder that Irish folk came over to help with the potato harvest. The site also had a pond and wooden buildings which were the property of the tenant Mr John Harrison ('The Goose King'

– hence the pond!). He paid a rent of £237 5s. (£237.25) per annum. There was a tithe rent of £19 5s. 5d. (£19.27) per annum. The tenure was freehold and the sale of the ground rent was withdrawn at £4,100.

LOT 51 – Gorse Hill Farm (100 acres) on the north side of New Cut Lane. The tenant was Mr Miles R. Blundell and he paid a rent of £223 a year with an annual tithe rent of £17 1s. (£17.05). With his 4-bedroomed house, he had 3 pigsties, a shippon for 28 cows, a barn, a six-stall stable, a mixing room and 3 loose boxes. Other buildings belonged to the tenant. The tenure was freehold and the sale of the ground rent was withdrawn at £4,800.

The package included the ground rents and freehold reversions of no fewer than eight pubs on the former Scarisbrick estate. Ormskirk brewers Ellis Warde bought the ground rents of The Swan at Bescar, The Ship at Haskayne and The Blue Bell at Barton. Other sales related to The Morris Dancers, The Red Lion, Scarisbrick, The Scarisbrick Arms at Downholland and The Saracen's Head at Halsall, where Ellis Warde, Webster & Co. of Ormskirk held the lease. The licensee was John Kenyon and the ground rent was £75.

At The Scarisbrick Arms, the lease was held by Greenall, Whitley and the licensee was William Tebbutt. The annual amount payable was £80. Mr T. Makinson of Birkdale bought it for £1,800. The accommodation included 6 bedrooms and an 8-horse stable, 2 loose boxes and a trap shed and garden.

The total raised in the sale was between £19,000 and £20,000, and 15 lots were withdrawn, representing, it was said, 'a fairly large sum'.

The Ormskirk Advertiser marked the occasion with an editorial saying that the sale had been the 'final severance of the Marquis de Casteja with his West Lancashire properties'. A couple of years previously, the Marquis had disposed of the vast proportions of his Scarisbrick, Halsall and Downholland estates. The celebrations when the present Marquis had attained his majority and when he had been happily married were recalled as the editorial continued: 'Everything went on happily until war broke out. Regarding this estate, as has been the case in scores of others, the war altered matters materially and the climax came when the Marquis made that dramatic announcement at the rent audit at Scarisbrick Hall which was only the forerunner of the later and now final sale of the whole estate'.

A few weeks previously, Scarisbrick Hall had been sold back to a Scarisbrick – Sir T. Talbot-Scarisbrick of Greaves Hall, Banks. The first Marquis, who married Lady Eliza Scarisbrick and died in 1899, was mentioned, as was the 'late Marquis' who had died in 1911 and had 'proved himself a typical and considerate English squire, though a Frenchmen of high lineage'.

Now attractive residential accommodation.

'Along with many others,' said the paper, 'we cannot but regret the severance
of long and pleasurable associations with the Casteja family.'

The estates were again on the market thirty years later – 3,576 acres in
142 lots. 43 lots were sold before the sale and 100 were auctioned at the
Wheatsheaf, Ormskirk, on 21 May 1953. Lots not reaching the reserve price
were withdrawn. Total rental for the combined estate was put at
£9,540 11s. 11d. coming mostly from agricultural holdings including accommodation land. There was rent from 25 cottages. 'The majority of tenants,'
said the sale document, 'have been associated with the estate for many
generations.'

Five-and-a-half thousand acres of the land south and west of the church
was sold, in 1956, to the Church Commisioners. Although some houses
still bear the Casteja name, a local resident put the changed situation like
this: 'The family farms gradually disappeared, with the Church Commissioners favouring larger units. Farms were amalgamated and the farm houses
sold off as private houses. This also led to ditches being filled in and the
trees removed to make larger fields for the huge modern machines. The
old order had gone forever'.

The agent acting for the Commissioners has since confirmed the change
to larger units. Thirty-three farms have now been reduced to ten but, he
explains, the changes have come about not through the owners' policy but
because of the modern trends in farm management.[15]

CHAPTER FOUR

Tucked Away in an Unspoilt Corner

Here is the Church;
There is the steeple,
Here's the Parson,
And there are the People

Y OU CANNOT TALK LONG about Halsall without mentioning the
church. 'One of the oldest and most beautiful churches in the Diocese
of Liverpool' says *The Treasures of Lancashire*.[1] So much has been written
by experts that it would be better for those particularly interested in church
architecture to study one or other of the books or leaflets produced. The
beauty and capacity of the interior have prompted special comment. 'Its
fabric,' says C. W. Budden,[2] 'still affords a fascinating architectural study'.
The aim here is merely to highlight what appear to be rather special facts
or features.

The dedication is to St Cuthbert – Bishop of Lindisfarne – who died
in AD 687. The legend about his remains is well known in the area. 'He
gave his disciples charge that his body should not become a prey to the
Danes,' says W. T. Bulpit,[3] 'and so, about a century after his death, we
find the monks in Cumberland fleeing before the Danes to take his honoured
remains to Ireland'. Storms thwarted the Irish crossing and the body was
brought south, resting at Lytham, North Meols (present-day Churchtown)
and Halsall. St Joseph's, Woodlands Road, Ansdell, Lytham, has a picture
rescued from the former Upholland Seminary depicting the procession
escorting the coffin. Wherever the remains rested overnight, a cross was
erected and this led – it is said – to the establishment of churches like St
Cuthbert's, Halsall. It would not be difficult to list a line of St Cuthbert
churches across the country.

Cuthbert was a lovable saint. 'A man of extraordinary charm and practical
ability, who attracted people deeply by the beauty of his holiness,' says the
Penguin Book of Saints.[4] After the troubles, his bones were re-buried in
Durham Cathedral – also dedicated to him. The Halsall Church porch –
an ancient structure renovated – is surmounted by an effigy of the saint

The church is dedicated to St Cuthbert, whose effigy appears on the building.

holding King Oswald's head. When the shrine was opened, the King's head was found with Cuthbert's remains and he is, for that reason, remembered with Oswald. A niche north of the altar probably held a statue of Cuthbert and was, perhaps, removed in the 1650s during the Commonwealth.

If regard in which a building is held can be determind by the amount of money and effort spent on it, Halsall Church scores highly. Work has been done continously in almost every century. Originally, there was very little nave. The visitors' leaflet[5] considers that development – which is not thought, on the whole, to have spoilt the original structure – was in a number of stages, summarised as follows:

1. Simple building – chancel, porch, no aisles – date unknown but probably replacing Norman structure.

2. Around 1290 – addition of north aisles with 4 bays – chapels, tower and spire on south west part of the nave.

3. 1340–50 – removal of tower and spire and addition of south aisle.

4. Rebuilding of tower (partly with original material) at west end of nave – in the light of subsequent alterations, not particuarly successful. 'The lines of the tower,' says the leaflet, 'are not adapted to fit the high-pitched nave roof, nor is it sufficiently high to stand properly at the west end'.

Halsall Church.

5. Raising walls of nave.

6. New roofing.

7. Around 1370 – erection of chancel restored 1873 and 1886. Liverpool's first bishop – John Charles Ryle – preached at both services on 14 May 1886. Always with an eye for an appropriate text, he preached in the morning on Psalm 95 verse 6 'O come, let us worship and bow down before the Lord our maker'.

It is all reminiscent of Betjeman: [6]

> The Church's restoration
> In eighteen-eighty-three
> Has left for contemplation
> Not what there used to be.
> How well the ancient woodwork
> Looks round the Rect'ry hall,
> Memorial of the good work
> Of him who plann'd it all.

There was apparently a Norman building on the site – part of which can still be seen a few feet at the angle of the nave with possible traces under the present building – but no part of the present building, as we have seen, is older than fourteenth century.

After the chancel was built between 1345 and 1350, the intention was to re-model the nave – then barely thirty years old! There is a reminder here of how a national calamity affected places like Halsall. The Black Death restricted this fourteenth-century building work. 50,000 died in London; half of the country's 750,000 inhabitants were swept away. Between September 1349 and January 1350, 3,000 died to the north in Preston. To the south, in Liverpool, a certain William of Liverpool 'caused one third of the inhabitants of Everton to be brought to his house after death'. Presumably, he did a good line in cheap funerals.[7]

The involvement of Halsall in all this is highlighted by Joseph Pearce in his *Romantic Tales of Old Lancashire*.[8] His story starts with a wagon load of ladders and scaffolding, hauled by oxen and driven by Tim of Ormskirk, having difficulty in turning from Aughton Street into Church Street. Simon the Lounger helps Tim re-load and is recognised by Tim as an old soldier comrade from Crécy. The reunion spontaneously results in Simon boarding the wagon for the hour's journey to Halsall Church, where new walls are being built at the eastern end. They are around and beyond the recently-built chancel. Rector Richard de Halsall had commissioned the work – a customary sort of project in these parts at this time. Simon had been unemployed since the wars and, to his delight, the Master Mason offers him employment in placing the scaffolding poles into tubs of earth for the erection of the Gothic-style building. First news of the plague comes *via* a maid at Snape Farm. Anabil of the Water Mill had been found at dawn at Bangors Green smitten by bubonic plague. The terror flies from cottage to cottage. Masons die at their benches. The Master Carpenter is absent one morning and is found, on enquiry, to be a victim of the plague – as, indeed, are all his mates.

> Priest and peasant and lord,
> By the swift, soft stroke of the air;
> By a silent, inevitable sword,
> In plough-field or banquet, fall.

Amazingly, Simon survives and, even though work on the church ceases, he stays on as watchman, scraping moss off the neglected stones and digging ditches to take away flood water. As an old man, in 1400, after the advent of a new generation of craftsmen, he is present, with his comrade Tim, at the dedication of the western tower.

The church in the 1920s, from a contemporary postcard.

'Within the church,' says Budden[9] 'the principal interests are in the chancel.' It is 20 feet wide and 46 feet long. 'Most gloriously fourteenth-century!' says Budden. The apex of the hood mould of the great East Window has a hand held up in benediction. The hand is carved in flat relief on a large block of stone. It possibly has relics behind it. The choir stalls receive a lot of attention. There are six on each side – the south stalls being the oldest. Standing for services – the custom still for monks even when kneeling was introduced elsewhere – was a strain for the elderly. Misericords – the word comes from 'mercy' – were introduced. These were shelves placed on the undersides of the hinged choir stall seats. When turned up, they supported the occupant during the long periods of standing. Very much like 'our modern theatre seats', says C. W. Budden.[10] He draws attention at Halsall to the carvings on these misericords of subjects very 'reminiscent of the daily life and thought of the common people'.

Scenes represented include:

1. Two naked men wrestling – hardly what you would describe as church art!

2. Angels, supported by dragons, holding a key in each hand.

A spring-clean in the early days of Canon Bullough's ministry.

3. A venerable-looking bearded man's head.

4. A group of eagles.

5. A fox and goose – reminscent of many inn signs.

6. A winged and robed angel holding a book.

7. Two fighting dragons.

There are effigies on the south side of the chancel. Sir Henry Halsall who died in 1523 was founder of a chantry – a chapel set up by the gentry for the celebration of masses for the repose of the souls of their founders and their families. The tomb also contains the body of Henry's wife, Margaret, daughter of James Stanley, Bishop of Ely. The piscinas – basins for washing communion vessels – suggest that the church once had four chapels. The southern chapel is to the memory of the soldier son of Canon Blundell, murdered while giving a drink to a wounded enemy soldier during the Boer War.

The Founder's Tomb on the north wall of the chancel is considered by Budden as 'a particularly beautiful feature of the church'. In an arched recess, this altar tomb is surmounted by an alabaster effigy of the Rev. Richard Halsall, with his wife alongside him. He was Rector for the half century from 1513 to 1563. Wearing typical clerical dress, he is 'tonsured' – his head has been shaved – and he wears a long surplice, an almuce (fur-lined-hood) and fur tippet or stole. His feet rest on a carved dog. Richard Halsall is called The Founder presumably because the founding of the Protestant church dates from the time of his ministry. Because of the politics of the day, he must have been very much a Vicar of Bray, adapting skilfully to the stop-start changes brought about successively by Henry VIII, Edward VI, Mary and Elizabeth.

The 60-foot long nave added to the original chancel has five arcades of octagonal pillars dividing it from the north and south aisles. It was once separated from the chancel by a screen. This is a reminder that the nave was once used, rather like a present-day church hall, for less ecclesiastical purposes. Heaven is represented in the chancel; the nave is the people's part of the church. In these days of 'customer-friendly' worship it is good to let John Betjeman remind us that 'twas not always thus:

> The stone floor of the church is often covered with yew boughs or sweet-smelling herbs whose aroma is stronger if crushed under foot. Strong smells were a feature of medieval life. People did not wash much or change their clothes often, and the stink of middens must have made villages unpleasant places in hot weather.[11]

The churchwardens, who collected the rent for church lands, often also arranged for the brewing, in the nave, of church ales in the parish utensils. It could 'be consumed there by the jovial and contributory parishioners'. 'The parish church and the graveyard in which it was set,' say Hutton and Cook,[12] 'were the centre of village life, both mundane and spiritual. They were associated with the deepest human feelings, joy and sorrow as well as the pleasures of festivals and saints' days, especially the annual feast known as the Church Ale. This was held in the nave and was followed by dancing.' Church life has, perhaps, lost some of its charms!

The rood screen was surmounted by the rood loft. The rood was a cross or crucifix over the entry to the chancel often, as we have noted, with a screen beneath it and the rood loft over the top. Access to the loft was by the rood stair. No trace of the screen remains at Halsall, but the rood staircase and doorway are left – the stairway being in an octagonal turret. The rood loft was sufficiently wide to accommodate a small altar and A. W. Pugin [13] lists four uses for such a platform:

1. An elevated place from which to sing out the Gospel to the congregation.

2. The Passion of the Lord was sung from the roodloft; the gradual (psalms after the epistle) and other parts of the mass were chanted and there might well have been a small organ to accompany this music.

3. Lessons were read from here, and Holy Days announced.

4. On feast days, at Christmas and Whitsuntide, there were decorations with evergreens and lights.

Near to the chancel arch – high on the south wall of the nave – are clerestory windows. Three large windows were put high up in the south wall as early as 1520 to give light to the rood. 'Clearstory' or clerestory means the 'upper storey of the nave walls of a church pierced by windows',[14] and the Halsall windows provided light for mystery plays. Religious drama is nothing new!

The rood loft would also be a useful place in which to place someone to guard the jewels on the high altar, the relics on display and the bread and wine available for Passion Week. He could also keep an eye on gifts laid out near the Founder's Tomb.

The practices taking place on the rood screen were meant to disappear following the Reformation, but remote areas like Halsall were slow to recognise the Protestant practices of the newly established Church of England. Local landowners, usually magistrates, were often themselves committed Roman Catholics, and had little enthusiasm for prosecuting folk who wanted to maintain the Old Faith to which they secretly adhered – those who refused, as they put it, 'to take wine with the parson'. In more recent times, Halsall has maintained the use of the 1662 Book of Common Prayer longer than most other parishes.

Three features of the naves in all Anglican churches are the pulpit, the lectern and font.

'Politics and the pulpit', said Edmund Burke,[15] 'are terms that have little agreement. No sound ought to be heard in the church but the healing

The early- to mid-nineteenth-century font, Halsall.

voice of Christian charity.' It is doubtful if all clerics occupying St Cuthbert's pulpit abided by this advice. We are reminded on the visitor to two London churches. In one he found a pulpit in the nave; in the other there was a knave in the pulpit! But politics or no politics, there was a deliberate attempt to control the length of sermons. Halsall has one of the few remaining hour glasses in the pulpit! This utilitarian pulpit equipment gets more mention than the structure itself. Perhaps it is little more than a standard item from the ecclesiaistical equivalent of a mail order catalogue! But Bulpit manages a 'noble'.[16] The lectern gets even less mention, but Bulpit claims that the pillar supporting 'the stately font' is 'the most ancient piece of work in the church' The visitors' guide dates it as 'early English', dating from the reign of Henry III' (1216–72). Part of the base of the bowl and the supporting shaft are all that remain of what must have been a very handsome medieval font, probably replacing something of which these two old pieces are only a part. This is apparently a 'chaste font, very different from the fantastically sculpted fonts of Norman churches'.[17]

    The south aisle east window has fragments of ruby red glass from the Decorated Period – 1290 to 1350. This suggests it has been in the building since the earliest days. 'Where fourteenth-century glass is still in situ (which is rare), it is especially interesting,' says June Osborne [18] She quotes from Piers Plowman: 'Secure should thy soul be for to dwell in heaven'. It was a warning, she says, that it was wrong to think you could buy your salvation

'by purchasing pardons "come from Rome all hot", or perhaps by com-
missioning a window'! The west window of the north aisle also contains
old glass. The east window has five compartments and, at least, the tracery
is original.

The present choir vestry – a gabled building running north and south
and built into the angle of the tower and south aisle – was once a two-storey
grammar school, on the upper storey of which lived the schoolmaster.
Edward – brother of the then Rector/Squire was the founder. 'Thou hast
traitorously corrupted the youth of the realm in erecting a grammar school' [19]
is a charge that could well have been levied against him! The claim that
he repeated the exercise in nearby North Meols has been disproved.

Edward's involvement is recorded over the now blocked doorway in the
east wall – the Halsall arms and the inscription 'EH 1593'. There is some
Latin over the doorway into the church from the vestry. It reads: 'To
Edward Halsall who built and endowed this school be praise'. Recorder of
Liverpool in 1579 and Mayor in 1579 and 1586, Edward was also, at some
time, Chamberlain of the Exchequer in Chester. When he died in 1593,
he gave lands and property in Eccleston and other areas to provide an
annual income of £13 6s. 8d. for the maintenance of his school. It provided
education for poor boys nominated for places by The Select Vestry.[20]

In the former grammar school, Bulpit [21] claims to have found the parish
chest containing seventeenth-century accounts when wine for communion
and more convivial occasions was 2s. 4d. a gallon (less than 12 pence these
days!) Charcoal was bought – presumably at the same knock-down price
– to provide warmth for the priest, and there was a curious stone dish in
which it was burned. Registers date from 1606, but were not kept regularly
until 1660 at the accession of Charles II when the Anglican Church was
re-established. The book itself cost 8s. (40p) – and came from William
Grice in Ormskirk.

Through a painting by T. Turner,[22] we have an interesting indication of
the interior of Halsall Church in 1794. The picture was probably the
frontispiece to a novel. A kindly cleric is preaching on the Sunday before
Christmas to a lethargic and widely scattered congregation. The coat of
arms identifies the church. Because part of the chancel arch is filled in by
a gate, we see only the lower part of the east window through an opening
beneath the royal arms. The effect, as in so many churches of the time,
was to turn the nave into a separate meeting area. Particular attention is
paid to the ladies' light blue Sunday hats. One lady has 'a stiff naivete
about her which is eloquent,' concealing, 'one feels, a notable character.'
Men's hats hang on the pillars.

'The kindly doctor,' says writer Frank Davies who comments about the

Local people congregate outside the lych gate waiting for a wedding party to emerge from the church in the 1950s.

picture, is presumably Glover Moore, a local man and son of Nicholas Moore of Barton. His monument in the chancel designates him as 'M.A.'. It is claimed that the sermon being preached is denouncing the war with Napoleon, whose navy was defeated in that particular year at Brest, Moore apparently acquired the reputation of a sedition-monger – not the first of his kind in Halsall.

Most of the exterior of the church, says Pevsner,[23] dates from 1886. The Perpendicular octagonal spire with its square base and octagonal belfry and 126 foot tower is similar in format to those of Ormskirk and Aughton St Michaels. There are six bells and a clock. The sandstone is local of 'a quality very superior to the ordinary'.[24] Gargoyles are a particular feature. The word comes from the name of a specific dragon thought to haunt the area of the Seine at Rouen where he is held responsible for flooding. Using figures of monsters on the outside of churches was a device to drive off

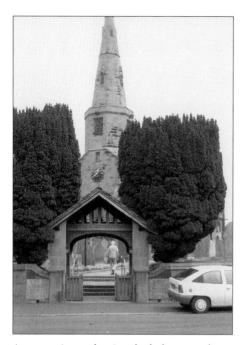

A recent picture showing the lych gate and, beyond, the octagonal spire of the church.

any of their kind who might threaten the building. Further protection came from ringing bells and hanging evergreens. Some of Halsall's twenty-four gargoyles have frightening faces – owls, bats, feathered fowls and fiends. But some are less grotesque. The lion, ox, eagle and man have been said to represent the four gospels. More likely, they are a potrayal of Revelation Chapter 4 verse 7: 'The first living creature was like a lion, the second was like an ox, the third had the face of a man, the fourth was like a flying eagle.' As footnote to this text, the NIV Study Bible, has the following note: 'Ezekial, in a vision, also saw four living creatures, each of whom had four faces – human in front, lion on the right, ox on the left, and eagle behind (Ezekial 1: 6, 10).'[25]

John's vision in the Book of Revelation was obviously influenced by this Old Testament reference. Our Halsall forebears knew their bibles! This particular craftsman, says Bulpit,[26] 'seems to have used his chisel wherever there was a coin of vantage for his work'. The man praying in a boat on the south buttresss of the chancel is a reminder that the sea once came much nearer to the village than it does now. Boats would often be in use at times of flooding and there was once a statue of St Nicholas – Patron Saint of Seafarers – looking out to sea from the west side.

In the vicinity of the walling north of the church with three doorways and windows, there is thought to have been a priest's house.

'Tucked away in an unspoilt corner of the Liverpool Diocese,' says Kathleen Eyre[27] about the church, 'it comes as a pleasant shock to discover craftsmanship of such high quality.'

CHAPTER FIVE

The Cure of Souls[1]

There goes the parson, oh! illustrious spark, And there, scarce less illustrious, is the clerk! [2]

THE ROLE AND CIRCUMSTANCES of Anglican parsons have very much changed since the first appointment to Halsall. Before the standard-isation of clergy pay, Halsall was a 'good living' and, therefore, 'a good catch', a fact highlighted by the number of occasions when the ruling family had one of their members in the job.

Robert is the first recorded Rector[3] and we find that he was in post about 1190, just after the Norman period. Richard I Coeur de Lion (the Lionheart) was king. It was at the time of the Crusades. Robert appears to have had connections with the newly founded Premonstratensian Cockersand Abbey in the Lancaster area. What 'followed the Norman Conquest [says Stephen Neill][4] was of advantage both to the English Church and to the nation with the spiritual care of which it was charged. This was the period [he says] of the first great reform of the Western Church after its emergence from the confusion of the Dark Ages'. With the Cockersand connections, Halsall seems to have been caught up in these national reforms!

Gilbert was the next Rector – in post from 1253 to 1266 – and he too was a Cockersand man. A new monastery with a desire to evangelise neighbouring areas? However, by the end of his ministry, Gilbert de Halsall had come on the scene and we see the advent of a particular feature of Halsall – members or friends of the ruling family being installed at the local church. The start of the 'Jobs for the Boys' syndrome!

William de Cowdray – rector from 1292 to 1296 – was a member of a minor Norman family whose earliest known ancestor was Jordan, Chamber-lain of Coudray. 'A chamberlain in the Middle Ages,' says Richard Ball Howard,[5] 'was one who presided over the household of the sovereign or a great nobleman, a service which he may have performed for the courts of Coudray in Normandy, and from whom the name would have been adopted.' In King John's day, the Coudrays built their manor house on

the present-day site of Meols Hall, Churchtown. The presence in Halsall
of a rector with such connections must have been an asset!

Gilbert de Halsall's next appointment – in November 1307 – was Henry
de Lea. His father, with the same name, was clerk at Down Holland. The
first Halsall on the scene is in February 1336. Richard, son of Thomas, is
presented by Gilbert as a replacement for Henry de Lea. He is the first of
seven Halsalls to hold the living. The last was Richard, appointed in June
1594. So anxious was the family to keep its finger on church affairs that
some members were appointed while still under age.

Richard de Halsall's replacement was not a family member, Uncharacter-
istically, the appointment was allowed to lapse. Was the family and the
whole area so devastated by the Black Death that they could not get round
to making an appointment? Because of the lapse, the Bishop stepped in
and Roger Milngate and John Spencer were appointed. In 1365, Pope
Innocent VI also gives Milngate the role of a notary.

By 22 December 1395, however, the Halsalls are back in the saddle. Even
though he is only 19, Henry de Halsall gets special papal dispensation for
his appointment. And his early start stands him in good stead; he goes on,
in 1413, to be Archdeacon of Chester – a move that seems to be an exchange
rather than an appointment. The Archdeacon of Chester since 1390 –
William de Neuhagh – comes to Halsall in Henry's place. He has a good
pedigree – a prependary of Lichfield before going to Chester.

Again, does Halsall illustrate, at parish level, features of the contemporary
church? There is every indication from his name that William de Neuhagh
was a foreigner. Significantly, Stephen Neill [6] says of the fourteenth-century
church:

> At York in the fourteenth century, less than half the cathedral appointments
> were held by Englishmen; at Salisbury fourteen out of twenty-one non-resident
> canons were foreigners. It is not surprising that in 1307 the parliament of
> Carlisle protested against the 'unbridled multitude' of papal 'provisions', by
> which unwanted foreigners were thrust into positions in the English Church.

But when Neuhagh died in 1426, we were back to the 'home brew',
even though the new rector was, again, under age. With a Bachelor of
Divinity degree at the age of 20, Gilbert de Halsall was given papal
dispensation to assume full responsibilities from the age of 22. He is still
there until his death, before he is 50, and probably Edmund Farrington's
appointment of a replacement is another example of doing a favour for a
friendly local family. Was he a Leyland Farrington? Whoever he was, he
stayed 43 years, giving way, in 1495, to another Halsall minor.

Hugh Halsall was only 19. Nicholas Gartside, whose turn it was to make the appointment, had offered the job to James Straitbarrel. But Henry de Halsall had 'jumped the gun' and appointed his son Hugh who, on his institution, had to pay Staitbarrel compensation of £20 a year for five years. The Archdeacon absolved him of all risks of excommunication for the irregularity which had occurred. This was, perhaps, as well – he died when only 37!

We have already met Richard Halsall – instituted 1513 – when we looked at The Founder's Tomb. Richard was Rector for most of the tumultuous half-century ever experienced by the Church, both locally and nationally. His will povided for his tomb, thus making him Halsall's most famous Rector – 'The Founder'. £20 was to be distributed at the funeral. Cousin John was given £100 'towards his exhibition at learning whereby executors shall appoint'. Nephew Henry got a John the Baptist brooch and his 'servant and curate' a whole year's wages and other bequests. The residue was for 'such alms, deeds or works of mercy, and charity' as his executors judged best. Melling and Maghull chapels got money for repairs and for a chalice. Assets left also included some valuable plate.

Perhaps at that time unsympathetic to Elizabeth's Protestant reforms, Richard refuses to appear at the 1562 visitation when there is an annual inspection and the swearing in of the parish officers. Things are a little better three years later when Cuthbert Halsall has taken over. He, at least, appears by proxy.

George Hesketh was instituted in 1571. (Was he a Hesketh of Rufford?) He was 'no preacher'. In contrast, Richard Halsall (1594) was 'a preacher'. When Richard (instituted 1594 and the last of the Halsall parsons) died, there were particular difficulties. The replacement, in 1633, was Peter Travers BD and he illustrates a particular evil of the Church of England which extended until the late nineteenth century. As well as holding the living of Halsall, Travers also held Bury. Although the period covered is slightly later then the time of Travers, Harold Nicholson[7] reminds us of the greed called 'plurarism':

> In 1806 there were as many as 2,423 parishes in which the incumbent was not resident. Nor did the higher clergy set a better example. The Bishop of Winchester, for instance, only visited his diocese once in twenty years. There thus arose delays in ordination and confirmation, and one bishop had to deal with the accumulation caused by his own absenteeism by confirming as many as eight thousand applicants in a single day.

Halsall was part of these alarming statistics. As part of the Diocese of Chester, extending as far as Cumberland, it is doubtful if they saw much of their bishop.

Travers was an ardent royalist and was one of the party with the Countess of Derby in the famous 1644 siege of Lathom Hall. This led to the publication, on 24 April 1645, which read:

> Whereas Peter Travers, Rector of the Parish of Bury, in the County of Lancaster, is disaffected to the Parliament and the proceedings thereof, and is in Lathom House, now kept a garrison against Parliament, it is ordered that the said rectory be forthwith sequestrated from the said Peter Travers.

For a few months, Nathaniel Jackson was the Halsall replacement but, on 13 December 1645, Thomas Johnson 'Minister of the Word' was installed. From Rochdale, Johnson was described as a 'godly and orthodox divine who is hereby required forthwith to officiate the cure of the Church as rector and preach diligently to the parishioners there'. Johnson was obviously sympathetic to the presbyterian bible-based approach of the Commonwealth. But the new regime was not unmindful of Mrs Travers whose husband had lost his livelihood. She received £20 *per annum* – a tenth of the tithes of the living – for her maintenance and that of the children. By now the job was worth £200 *per annum* but the parson 'by corruption' had 'put £30 on it' – meaning, presumably, that it was worth less than it used to be.

Because of the mismanagement of the Lord of the Manor – Cuthbert Halsall – the estate had been sold to Lord Gerard. He appointed the next rector. The date was 20 February 1660 – three months before the Restoration – and the appointee was Matthew Smallwood BD. He was another plurarist, with a living in Gawsworth, Cheshire, with which the Halsall patron had connections. He was also a prebendary of St Paul's and Lichfield, where he is buried.

It seems likely that the parish was neglected. Smallwood's successor – probably his curate – was Nathaniel Brownell, an Oxford MA. 'An active and careful man; the restorer of both the church and the school,' says the write-up. He had a faculty for teaching boys, no doubt, in the grammar school.

William III had landed at Torbay on 5 November 1688 and James II had sped to France. 'With him,' says Stephen Neill,[8] 'went Old England that was never to come again.' The Glorious Revolution had arrived and 9 bishops and 400 clergy found that, having sworn allegiance to James, they could not, in their consciences, take an oath to another monarch. The form of words did not help: 'I AB do sincerely promise and swear to bear true allegiance to Their Majesties, King William and Queen Mary'. The problem was the absence of 'lawful and right'. But the new Rector of Halsall – Matthew Brownell – did not have a problem. In 1689, he is listed as 'conformable'. He was rector for 36 years – the sort of stability the parish needed after its recent 'ups-and-downs'!

With the next vacancy, Peter Walker, now with the power to grant the living, found it necessary for some reason to do what had happened in 1413 – foreigners were appointed. Albert de Blanc came in 1719, and David Cromarque eleven years later. Both had Cambridge associations.

Harold Nicholson [9] says of the Church of England at this time that 'there was an utter absence of religious fervour or conviction, and Goldsmith [10] denounced even the better types of clergymen for their 'inspired calmness'. There was little (says Nicholson) in the parish church, or even the cathedral, 'to arouse the interest or the emotions of the faithful'.

Our Turner picture of the interior of Halsall Church – drawn half a century later than the Blanc/Cromarque period and mentioned earlier – certainly confirms that impression. If these incumbents were not entirely fluent English speakers, the situation could have been even worse than the norm!

A four-year stint by one Edward Pilkington followed. Judging by the name, he was probably a local candidate, as was his successor Dr John Stanley, brother of Sir Edward Stanley, 7th Earl of Derby. The good doctor seems, at the same time, to have been Rector of Winwick. Charles Mordaunt was now patron. Having appointed a member of a local family with whom he was apparently on good and profitable terms, in 1757, he put in Henry Mordaunt – a member of his own family. He was 25 at the time but died when he was 50 by falling from his horse. He replacement was local man 22-year-old Glover Moore, already mentioned in connection with the Turner picture. He was in dispute with tenants because of his imposition of a tithe tax on potatoes.

When Colonel Morduant sold the estate to the Scarisbricks, possibly because the new owners were Roman Catholics, the Colonel sold the giving of the living to Jonathan Blundell of Liverpool. It has been in this family's ownership ever since and, like the Halsalls and the Mordaunts, they have been able to appoint members of their own family as incumbents. Thomas Blundell was an Oxford graduate, but his successor in 1816 – Richard Loxham – was from Cambridge. He had previously been at St John's, Liverpool. Richard Leigh followed in 1843 and he went on ultimately to Walton-on-the-Hill.

We are now in 1863 and Thomas Blundell is appointed. We can be excused for dwelling at some length on his life and times. He is one of the notable Rectors of the parish and his life – which coincides almost exactly with that of Queen Victoria (whom he served, at one stage, as an honorary chaplain) – saw tremendous changes in state and church.

Above: An interesting view from the church spire shows the gates before the construction of the lych gate and a quiet semi-rural scene beyond.

Opposite: Canon Blundell died in 1905, and his funeral seems to have attracted a lot of attention from pioneering photographers.

Thomas Blundell Hollinshead Blundell was, in every sense, a typical Victorian parson.[11] His birth very much coincided with the passing of the 1832 Reform Act which affected the way MPs were elected and swept away a lot of ancient privileges. Slavery was abolished about the same time but, in 1834, The Tolpuddle Martyrs were transported. Morse developed the telegraph and a regular steamship service began across the Atlantic. The Penny Post was introduced and the first co-operative store was established. In an Oxford still reeling from the defection of John Henry Newman to the Church of Rome as Blundell was preparing for his MA, Charles Darwin wrote his controversial *On The Origins of Species*. 'Is man an ape or an angel?' asked Disraeli.[12] 'Now I am on the side of the angels!'

As he does his one-year spell as a curate at St Michael's, Handsworth under the guidance, significantly, of the Rev. Charles Mordaunt, the London Underground is being built. As he moves very quickly to the 'valuable family living of Halsall' offered him by his brother, William Booth is founding the Salvation Army. State education is introduced in Blundell's early days in Halsall; women are admitted to Cambridge for the first time; the telephone is now avaialble as are Daimler's petrol-driven engines; electric trams are introduced in Blackpool.

Thomas Blundell lived throughout the Crimean War, The American Civil War and The Boer War. It was in this war that his son was killed caring for an enemy soldier – a death that hastened his wife's death and ruined his own health.

By the time of Thomas Blundell's arrival, the £4,000 a year Halsall stipend, coming from tithes and rents, had been reduced by commitments in establishing the parishes of Melling, Lydiate and Maghull. He voluntarily gave up other income to help struggling parishes in Crossens and Banks. The new school ('perfect from a sanitary and modern aspect in every detail'),[13] which opened shortly after his death, owed its 'inception to his influence'. He served on the Lancashire Education Committee. The restoration of the church buildings, in 1873 and 1886, were his projects.

A total abstainer, Canon Blundell built 'well-fitted cocoa rooms near the church'. He was a prominent freemason. He died, unexpectedly, on All Saints Day (1 November), 1905, after an operation in London. 'The father of his people', said one of the tributes, 'the ever-ready of the poor and needy and a source of real joy to all those who came in contact with him.' Archdeacon Madden underlined the changed conditions which had come about during his lifetime and to which we have already referred. 'There

Charles Robert Claxton (Bishop of Warrington as well as Halsall's Rector) with comedian Norman Evans at the Rose Queen Ceremony in Coronation Year.

Canon Bullough revived the custom of blessing the crops at Rogationtide.

are few clergymen,' he said, 'of the old-fashioned school which he represented now left – the courtliness of manner, with consideration for others, with steadiness of disposition'. Canon Blundell was said to have an 'enthusiasm that was inspiring'.

He left three children – Cuthbert Halsall, Mrs Alston – wife of Mr A. Alston of Bedfordshire – and Hilda Blundell who lived in the village afterwards and continued to be involved in church matters.

More recent appointments have been:

James Gerard Leigh – 1906 to 1921;

George Hardwicke Spooner – 1921 to 1928;

Edward Leigh Mather – 1928 to 1946.

Rector Spooner combined the post with that of Archdeacon of Liverpool and later also took on the role of Chancellor of the developing cathedral. At a ceremony on 17 February 1925 in Church House, Liverpool, he received

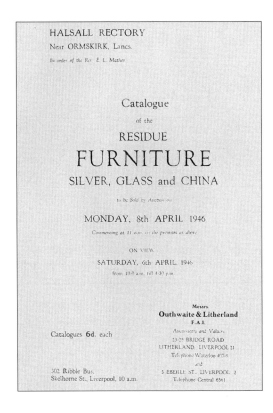

HALSALL RECTORY
Near ORMSKIRK, Lancs.
By order of the Rev. E. L. Mather

Catalogue
of the
RESIDUE
FURNITURE
SILVER, GLASS and CHINA
to be Sold by Auction on

MONDAY, 8th APRIL 1946
Commencing at 11 a.m. on the premises as above

ON VIEW
SATURDAY, 6th APRIL, 1946
from 10-0 a.m. till 4-30 p.m.

Messrs.
Outhwaite & Litherland
F.A.I.
Auctioneers and Valuers
23-25 BRIDGE ROAD
LITHERLAND, LIVERPOOL 21
Telephone Waterloo 4078
and
3 EBERLE ST., LIVERPOOL 2
Telephone Central 6561

Catalogues 6d. each

302 Ribble Bus,
Skelhorne St., Liverpool, 10 a.m.

a presentation in recognition of his fifty years' ministry in the Diocese. He had served under all the bishops since Bishop Ryle, coming from Oxford to All Saints, Great Nelson Street, followed by Litherland, Woolton and currently Halsall. At 73, he was 'the friend of everybody and Father of Church House'.

Rector Mather was a former curate of Halsall and had left for Hornby on the arrival of Rector Spooner. His Halsall incumbency included the period of the Second World War. He was well respected in the parish and the Mathers' loss of a son in the war was a grief shared by everyone.

On his retirement, Mr Mather had a sale of surplus furniture. It was held on Monday 8 April 1946,[14] and nearly 400 items ranging from axminster stair carpet to a Royal Doulton Breakfast Service, a Valuable Canteen of Cutlery by Goldsmiths & Silversmiths Ltd, to a Gilt Framed Chippendale Triple Glazed Firescreen and from a Medici Print of 'The Last Supper' to an Antique Period Armchair were put under the hammer.

Rector Mather was replaced by Edward Ord Hunter, who only stayed two years. Charles Robert Claxton was instituted on 18 December 1948, combining his parish work with the role of Bishop of Warrington. He left Halsall to become Bishop of Blackburn and was succeeded by Walter Herbert Bullough who came from another 'Blundell living' and retired in 1991. Because of unsuccessful attempts to amalgamate livings, it was 1994 before the appointment of the present rector – Canon Peter Goodrich.

Halsall, then, has had 38 Rectors since 1190. The average pastorate is, therefore, 21 years – comparing very favourably with the 5–7 years modern churchgoers can expect to have from their clergy. But this, as we have said, is not surprising.

CHAPTER SIX

Desirable Residences

Houses are built to live in and not to look on; therefore let use be preferred before uniformity, except where both may be had.[1]

H AVING LOOKED AT THE CHURCH and the school and those who directed the affairs of the village in matters both secular and spiritual, we can now ask 'Where did the folk live who attended church and school and were under the jurisdiction of the powers that be?'

Baines[2] gives an 1821 figure of 108 houses accommodating 115 families. As in many country districts, the church was obviously too large for the needs of the immediate vicinity. But there were originally all five townships for St Cuthbert's to serve. There was not much thought given to the problems faced particularly by poor folk in getting their dead to the parish church for the funeral and burial. 'The builders were chiefly concerned with making the interior of the church as rich and splendid as possible, something to bring you to your knees,' says John Betjeman.[3] Speaking of the fifteenth century, he goes on to say: 'The church is so prominent because the equivalents of cottages in the village are at the grandest "cruck houses" ... and most are mere hovels. They are grouped round the church and manor house and look rather like a camp.'

This could well have been the impression gained on a visit to medieval Halsall – a number of cottages fairly widely scattered. The Hearth Tax of 1666[4] shows that very few houses in the parish had as many as three hearths.

Figures have been calculated for 1824 rural labourers' wages.[5] They averaged 8–10 shillings. In some southern counties, they were as low as 4s. 6d. but, surprisingly perhaps, in Lancashire they are said to have been about 12s. By the 1890s, the average wage in West Lancashire had risen to 18–20 shillings. Rents seemed to have been about 1s. 6d. a week.[6] 'Boys left home for farm work or apprenticeships and girls went in to domestic service,' says John Burnett,[7] 'so relieving pressure on overcrowded cottage bedrooms. Lancashire [he continues], with its possibilities of relatively high earnings for young adults in the Cotton Industry, was a special case.'

But more substantial houses than those earlier cottages have since been built. The *Victoria County History*[8] gives a 1901 population of 1,236, based on a Halsall which does not now include Baines' townships and has Halsall, centred on the church and Shirdley Hill as the main centres of population. Before planning regulation days, many old houses will have been replaced, but the present-day system of listing buildings of special or historic interest has enabled the parish to preserve at least part of its heritage.[9]

Halsall Hall is opposite the school on the A5147. Because of its develop-ment recently as attractive appartment accommodation, it has been the subject of special expert study.[10] We got some idea of the use of the Hall in 1973 when the *Ormskirk Advertiser*[11] visited Councillor and Mrs Cropper – the third generation of the family to occupy what was then a New Street farm house and nerve centre of a 200-acre farm holding. Subsequently, John Bate[12] wrote: 'South-west Lancashire has many fine, old farmhouses, but perhaps one of the most striking is Halsall Hall,'

Built of brick, the hall is on solid rock, like the church, and has three storeys. Commissioned in the 1700s by Charles Lewis Mordaunt, it replaced an earlier structure. The Croppers recognised the existence of this earlier medieval house by giving place of honour to an octagonal stone. It was set into the structure near the back door. The Mordaunt connection is remembered by their coat of arms on the doorway into the courtyard. The initials CH on the front of the building are for Sir Cuthbert Halsall, Lord of the Manor in 1613. The stone is said to have been put into place by the Marquis de Casteja during his ownership of the estate – a pleasant gesture to a previous owner who would have been unknown to him. The title 'Halsall Hall' was assumed in the mid-nineteeenth century.

The cellars, already mentioned in connection with the Industrial Revol-ution use of the building, are carved into the rock. The craftsmanship used in their construction is very significant. There were mysterious staircases carved in stone. Rubble through which channels have been dug have yielded examples of late seventeenth-century pottery and a coin from the reign of William III (1695–1701). Above ground, the craftsmanship in many of the rooms is a reminder of the wealth of the Mordaunts. Labour costs in those days were no problem and the servants' quarters are part of the main building together with a bakehouse and laundry. Farm workers 'lived in'. Half the courtyard – a lawn in the 1970s – had once been the kitchen garden.

Was there once a a tunnel between the hall and the church? A local resident[13] provides this information: 'In 1728, the young Lord Cowper[14] came to visit Halsall because it had a famous grotto at the Hall.' Whether this was built under the Hall because there are blocked up tunnels there or in the grounds is not known. Lord Cowper wrote that 'The grotto is very pretty but, as for the country round about, it is now laid under water and looks like a little sea.'

The 1987 report on the building describes Halsall Hall as a five-bay (two storeys and an attic), 'single pile building lying on an approximately north–south axis'. Constructed of brick on a sandstone plinth with sandstone mullioned windows, quoins, string course and door dressings, it had a limestone flag roof. The building was probably designed for the multiple accommodation of family and staff and industrial use to which we have referred. The water mill between the church and the hall was demolished in 1880.

Carr Moss Lane is on the right going from Southport to Maghull shortly after passing Halsall Hall. Most of the property on the left is quite new – Linaker Drive Estate – is post-World War II. Just before what was the railway bridge on the right are some houses built at the beginning of the century. The sites would have become useful because of their proximity to the station. Halsall Station House, now with its white rendering, is still to be seen to the right. Poultry houses replaced the Altcar Bob (of which more later!). The house was the wartime HQ for the Home Guard.

On the other side of the road is an old cottage, its unhindered view across the fields now completely blocked by the road going over the railway bridge. This is possibly the oldest existing house in the parish. Beyond the bridge is an 1881 farm house. Holt Farm – further down the lane on the left – was built by the Harrisons from Melling and the farm house was the first to be built on reclaimed land.

Back on New Street, the A5147, and turning right towards Lydiate, are a number of the older houses. There are cottages on the corner. Number 58 is early nineteenth-century in brick with a slate roof. The style of the brickwork, with alternating stretchers and headers in each course, is known as Flemish Bond.[15] The plan for the house is described as 'double-depth'; there are three storeys and an attic and three bays. Sash windows have glazing bars and painted stone lintels and sills. The door in the middle bay has a fanlight rising within the open pediment of a Tuscan pilaster doorcase of painted stone or stucco. (For those of us who are uninitiated, a pilaster is a 'representation of a classical column in flat relief against a wall';[16] Tuscan suggests mouldings but no decoration). There are gable chimneys and light for the attic is via windows in the gable walls. The northern window is sashed and has Gothic style glazing.

Number 62 was repaired in 1880 at the time of the Marquis de Casteja, and Bank Cottage built in 1878 also bears his initials. He has certainly left his mark on the village. No. 80 also dates from 1878, while no. 86 is as early as 1773. The farm on the right just before the speed restriction signs has, at the rear, a 'shant' – 'one up-one down' house which accommodated Irish labourers who came over to help with the potato harvest.

Retracing our steps and into Halsall Road, the listed buildings list draws our attention to the war memorial outside the church gate erected in the 1920s and standing on a fifteenth-century base, and to three items near the church building:

The ruins known as Halsall Abbey, north-north-east of the church.

» An old octagonal font a metre SE of the church. It is early-to mid nineteenth-century and sandstone.

» A sundial 10 metres south of the church. This is again sandstone and dated about 1700 with a brass plate and arm that projects the shadow of the sun – items probably renewed this century.

» Ruins approximately 230 metres NNE of the church known as Halsall Abbey. Although what they represent does not conform to any obvious medieval plan, these are possibly the remains of a fouteenth-century priest's house altered in the eighteenth or nineteenth century. These ruins came to light when the area was cleared for public access in 1964 and historian Jennifer Lewis has provided a lot of detail about the buildings.[17]

The first reference to a rectory is in 1563 and, by 1660, the accommodation consists of a hall – probably containing spinning equipment – a great parlour and smaller ones and closets, larders, a brewhouse, a dairy, kitchen and study. These would have constituted a substantial group of buildings with the domestic quarters having at least two storeys. The complex developed further over the years and may well have ranged around three or four sides of a courtyard with its own gatehouse. There were three tithe barns – a reminder that inhabitants of Melling, Maghull and Lydiate as well as Halsall were required to give the rector 10% of their produce.

A 1907 artist's impression of what the original rectory might have looked like.

Halsall House, built by the Blundells, and set amid glorious parkland.

Jennifer Lewis suggests that the buildings were finally demolished in the mid-nineteenth century.

Beyond these ruins, in the same grounds, is Halsall House, built as a replacement rectory between 1847 and 1850 by Sydney Smirke for the Blundell family. Smirke has a number of ecclesiastical buildings in the area [18] – the church and parsonage at Bickerstaffe, the Earl of Derby's church of St James, Lathom and – further afield – Christ Church, Treales on the Fylde, plus work in Bury. Pevsner [19] says the Halsall building is 'dignified' and mentions the symmetrical entrance side with a Gothic loggia of 4-centred arches. Again the material is sandstone. A detailed list of features is available – Smirke seemed to favour Jacobean features; the SE turret and open-well staircase are in this style.

There is also a special feature in the grounds. A 'ha-ha' is defined as 'a sunk fence bordering a garden or park that allows uninterrupted views from within'.[20] It is said that the idea came originally from India but others claim that the word is eighteenth-century and based on the French word 'ha!' denoting surprise. This is a useful, inoffensive device restricting livestock

to a specific area. Clergy in the past would have been fairly self-sufficient in providing food for the rectory. Whatever its origin, this device has been used to the east, south and west of Halsall House. It was built in 1850 but has been altered since. Bridges in the centre now spoil what should have been an uninterrupted view of the house.

The entrance gateway to the grounds is also listed.

The third rectory stands in its own grounds across the main road and alongside the playing fields. It was built when Canon Blundell ceased to be rector. The Blundell family appear to have looked upon the building as their property despite changed circumstances and, no doubt, were instrumental in providing a replacement house. Halsall House was later owned by the Copes family – Copes was a famous Liverpool firm of tobacco dealers. A family called Spence then moved in and they were followed by the Spencers – said to have made their money by buying up the disused Liverpool Overhead Railway as scrap. An agent for the Church Commissioners called Brett is then said to have bought the house for his own use.

The last rector to live in the replacement rectory was Canon Bullough

West Lancashire vernacular: Pemberton Farm, Northmoor Lane.

Cottages in Morris Lane.

– appointed in 1959. There were long discussions with the Diocese after his retirement about accommodation for the new incumbent and these, together with suggestions that Halsall living might be amalgamated with a neighbouring parish, lengthened the interregnum.

Beyond the 'Blundell' rectory – towards Scarisbrick – is a distinctive white house once called Greenways. It was built by folk associated with the Southport estate agents Ball and Percival and then occupied by members of the Moores (Littlewoods Pools) family. The churchyard contains the grave of Kathleen Ann Moores, wife of David Moores, who died at 26 when her car ran into a ditch on Haskayne Moss.

The present Rector lives at Gesterfield Farm on the the left of the A5147 going towards Scarisbrick and before reaching Gregory Lane. At the other end of the village, 'The Hermitage' at the corner of Plex Lane and the main road was once the curatage until Chestnut Cottage in Summerwood Lane took over this role.

Reg Calland, living in one of the low houses at the corner of Gregory Lane, was a regular Southport Flower Show winner. It is worth going further towards Scarisbrick and turning into Morris Lane where, near White House Farm, there are some delightful barn conversions at right angles to the road. Northmoor Lane has a house dated 1752 on the left before you reach the canal bridge.

We go back to the church. Across the road from the church and pub is The Runnel – a cul-de-sac flanked by fields of heavy clay. There was once a brick kiln in the field on the right and a big hole exists from which clay was taken. Further down is the start of a branch canal – never completed – which was to have linked with the Leeds and Liverpool Canal to facilitate the transport of bricks and farm produce.

The pub was once The Scarisbrick Arms – a bit odd to be named after the neighbouring parish. This was put right latterly; it became The Halsall Arms. Prior to 1828, the building was part of the Scarisbrick Estate. The records of the previous owners, Greenalls,[21] show that Edward Culshaw of Scarisbrick, yeoman, sold a plot of land in Halsall on 2 June 1835 'upon which lately stood a house and outbuildings belonging to John Harrison's tenement, and a dwelling-house and outbuildings erected and built on the plot of land and now in the occupation of James Pye as tenant'. Further transfers of the property are as follows:

12 July 1842 – William Leak sold to Richard Tyrer of Formby, gentleman:
Dwellinghouse now used as a public house called the 'Scarisbrick Arms' together with stables, brewhouse and outbuildings in the occupation of John Thomson as tenant.

20 August 1874 – Trustees of the late Richard Tyrer [then described as a brewer] sold to John Hulme Robinson of Southport, gentleman:
The Scarisbrick Arms public house as before.

19 December 1876 – William Hogarth of Preston, retired chemist and druggist sold his interest in the Scarisbrick Arms public house (after a mortgage) to Richard Whitehead Richardson and William Richardson of Rainford, brewers.

6 May 1884 – Executors of the will of Richard Whitehead Richardson sold his interest in the property to William Richardson.

13 April 1893 – William Richardson, brewer, sold the property to Greenall Whitley & Co. The house was then held on an original lease of 1828 based on three lives.

10 September 1894 – A new lease was granted to Greenall Whitley & Co. Ltd by the Marquis de Casteja of Scarisbrick Hall for a term of 60 years. The property was then a hotel and premises known as the Scarisbrick Arms together with parcels of land, and there was a clause in the lease whereby the company had to alter and improve the property within the first six months.

16 December 1932 – The company purchased the freehold of the property.

The cellars are a reminder that, like the church and Halsall Hall, the foundations are built upon a rock. Until the building of Halsall Waterworks, the pub had its own supply of spring water and prided themselves on the coolness of their beer. Once a centre of activity during the coursing season, the Scarisbrick Arms had a predecessor in some cottages – still there – behind the church. The most famous Scarisbrick Arms landlord was called Tebbutt. His meals were first class, prompting the view that he had once been in a large hotel or in the service of a gentleman's house.

But, alas, the pub is no more! The building began to fall into disrepair about 1996 and was a regular target for vandals. Plans to bulldoze it to make way for seven houses were said by the press [22] to have been 'slammed by local residents'. It was said to be 'outrageous' that companies based outside the village should continually try to get planning permission for housing, no matter what the consequences for the village. One resident of eighty years' standing urged the brewery to restore the pub to its former glory but, in the event, mine host has given way to a financial adviser. Where pints were once drawn, they now draw up balance sheets. 'Save and Prosper' has replaced 'Eat Drink and be Merry!' Richard Barber, Independent Financial Advisers, have replaced landlord and barmaid!

The road running between the church and the former pub is called Summerwood Lane. Number 3A, housing the post office and seen properly

The post office is housed in a listed building.

The original telephone exchange was in the post office. This is the future postmaster Arthur Mawdesley with his mother.

by going round the corner past the public entrance, is an early nineteenth-century house using the Flemish bond style and slate roof and double-depth plan seen in New Street. It is, in fact, very similar in style to 58 New Street and has a 6-panel door within a stone pilaster doorcase with a fanlight and open pediment. The Mawdesleys kept the post office. Arthur was church sexton and rang the bell; his sister ran the post office and also

An old view of Summerwood Lane. The building on the left is the former Cocoa Rooms and the one adjoining it was William Deacon's Bank.

manned the telephone switchboard. When all the Mawdesleys died, the village was without a post office.

Then the Burgesses – two brothers – bought the station house and goods yard. Poultry sheds were erected and eggs were sold on a large scale. But one of the brother's wives found room in one of the buildings for a post office. Other items such as sweets were also sold. But after a few years, the post office was back in its original location.

Modern houses have been built on the site, behind the church, of the tithebarn which was later the school and the St Cuthbert's Hall. In this area was 'Hearse House' so named because it housed the bier used by the church for funerals. The house was later used for club rooms for the youth club. There are quite a number of new houses along the lane presumably using up available plots and replacing older properties. The number of such properties increased as sewerage facilities were extended. But there are three older and distinctive houses at the beginning of the lane on the right-hand side. The white house standing back from the road – no. 8 – once housed the Cocoa Rooms kept by Annie and Jane Guy. They sold toffee, pop and cigarettes. Children preferred to be served by Annie; she was more generous in her portions. The District Bank also had a room in the building. The Tontine Club also met there. A Tontine was a mutual insurance scheme to which members subscribed each week; it was often referred to in Lancashire as 'The Diddle-'Em Club'. Friendly societies of this sort were very much in vogue at the time of Lloyd George, when it was thought that new social legislation would operate within membership of such organistaions.

Number 9 is the double-fronted Chestnut Cottage; at one time, home for the curate.

Further along the lane on the left is Glebe Farm (the glebe was the land surrounding the church from which the parson obtained an income), once having a milking herd providing supplies for the milk round operated by the Oswalds. What is now S. G. Seeds was built during the Second World War as a hostel for the Women's Land Army. As we get nearer to the canal, there are half a dozen houses on the right built in the early part of the century and possibly there because their occupants had some involvement with the canal. There was a cottage very close to this site where the first sod was cut for the canal. Traffic on the canal led to its enlargement so that it could be used as a waterside warehouse. No doubt refreshment was provided from an early date but it was 1872 before the first licence of the then 'Saracen's Head' was obtained. One wonders why a title with Arabic, nomadic rather than nautical associations was chosen! The present bar is said to be in the area of the original cottage and there is now a Watergate Bar overlooking the canal. The 7-foot high ceilings, distinctive beams and antique brass and copperware give everything a distinctive atmosphere – an attractive venue for pub lunches! Kenyons – parents of a well-known vet practising in Princes Street, Southport – are associated with the pub, as is Hugh Sharrock who pioneered the local provision of motor taxis and coaches. An Everton supporter, Hugh Sharrock was not likely to serve customers wearing red! The pub has traditionally been the meeting place for The Oddfellows.

When passenger traffic on the canal ceased with the coming of the railway, there was a storage site in the vicinity for manure brought out of Liverpool for the fertilising of countryside fields. The area must have had a very distinctive smell about it! Beyond the Saracen's Head, over the bridge, – Warehouse Bridge – are houses originally accommodating some of the skilled workmen/craftsmen of the village. The listed buildings document also draws attention to the early wedge-shape nineteenth-century boundary stone with neighbouring Scarisbrick on Pinfold Lane.

A report in 1925 by the County Medical Officer about some property in West Lancashire,[23] is a reminder that Halsall property was not as attractive as it is now. Presumably the houses mentioned were discovered after spot checks or as a result of complaints. In Plex Lane, a one-storey cottage is cited. Does the name Pilkington in brackets indicate the tenant? Among other deficiencies, the privy is dilapidated and is close to the house. In Cheapside, there are two thatched cottages where the water supply comes from a dip well liable to pollution in cultivated land. There is also a single-storey thatched cottage with damp in the front bedroom and a back bedroom which is decayed and useless. In Morris Lane, there are four old semi-detached two-storey cottages and each of the four dwellings has a privy and midden, and two of which have dilapidated structures. Gettern Cottages are two one-storey cottages without back doors. In contrast, in New Street, a block of three houses (occupants Edwards?) are in a fair state of repair. It is, perhaps, not without significance that, three months after the above report, the Rector of Halsall – speaking in Ormskirk at The Archdeacon's Visitation – an event attended by churchwardens and sidesmen from the whole area – chose to highlight the state of housing in West Lancashire. Relating it to other difficulties, the Archdeacon said:[24]

> The other problem was that of more adequate and up-to-date housing in rural districts, where in many cases the structural condition and accommodation for mixed families were deplorable in the extreme, and defying all claims of convenience, comfort, decency and morality.

The timing of these remarks was interesting. 'With the breaking up of many of the large territorial estates in parts of West Lancashire,' said *The Ormskirk Advertiser* in response to the Archdeacon's remarks, 'there has followed a deplorable lack of the erection of cottage property'[25] – a reminder that, until now, it had only been the estates that, because of their monopoly position, could provide property for rental.

The Archdeacon Rector of Halsall would have been well aware of the publicity given to World War I veterans told of Homes Fit for Heroes – 'You cannot expect to get an A1 population out of C3 homes'.[26] The 1924 Housing Act piloted through by John Wheatley, 'architect of the Labour-Catholic Alliance', offered increased subsidies to local authorities. But, even when land in Halsall became available, West Lancashire seems to have resisted the sort of changes brought about when Lord Derby's Knowsley estate was made available for massive Liverpool overspill housing schemes. If the Mordaunt's cotton manufacturing enterprise had continued, the development of Halsall might have been very different. If land in Halsall had fallen into other hands, we might, similarly, have been a different type of area than we know today. What probably saved the day was the value of the agricultural land, which led to tight planning controls: the lack of sewerage provision also held up the provision of more houses. Presumably, the only development to come out of the drive for more housing was the Linaker Estate in Carr Moss Lane.

History repeated itself in 1979 when the then Rector, Canon Herbert Bullough said:

> Few couples I have married in the past twenty years have managed to find a home here because of the planning retrictions. The only new development during my ministry has been the Georgian houses in Summerwood Lane and the occasional building of a bungalow or house at very high cost.[27]

Dick Ainscough's grandfather celebrating in the grounds of
Halsall Hall during the Jubilee of Queen Victoria.

CHAPTER SEVEN

The People, Lord, the People[1]

The Lord prefers common-looking people. That is why he makes so many of them.[2]

H AVING LOOKED at the Halsall 'powers-that-be' in Church and Manor House, what of those of humble origin? How did they earn their living? Who coped with their everyday needs?

In earlier days, for the reasons explained, the population would have been very small. Baines[3] adds the townships of Down Holland, Lydiate, Maghull and Melling to that of Halsall itself to form what he calls Halsall. As we are only concerned about the present-day parish of Halsall, the following population figures are those that interest us:

Population of the Township of Halsall:

1801	1811	1821
751	781	621

Why the drop in 1821? The other townships grew quite significantly:

Population of Downholland, Lydiate, Maghull and Melling

	1801	1811	1821
Downholland	482	552	970
Lydiate	532	614	691
Maghull	534	599	720
Melling	402	471	528

Could we make a guess why the Halsall figure fell so significantly? We have earlier discovered that Charles Mordaunt – Lord of the Manor – was very much involved in the cotton industry. He died in 1808 and his successors do not appear to have continued these activities. Could those involved in the venture – many of them actually living in part of Halsall Hall – have lost their jobs and accommodation and been forced to move to other areas – such as Maghull and Southport – where new enterprises were developing?

Of the total of 618 families in 1821 in the five townships, 319 (63%) were employed chiefly in agriculture, 160 (26%) in trade, manufactures and

Hughie Sharrock, one-time landlord of the Saracen's Head, pioneered the local bus service.

handicraft and the remaining 67 (11%) in professional pursuits or (and Baines obviously feels this amounts to the same thing as being a professional!) 'unemployed'.

Those classed as being in trade include James Barton (corn miller), Roger Barton (grocer), Richard and Samuel Park (maltsers), James Halton and John Kirby (blacksmiths), Thomas Blundell and J. Watkinson (saddlers). The state of the roads kept three wheelwrights busy – W. Aspinwall, Adam Glover and Thomas Park, and there are three Halsall pubs listed – The Loggerheads (Richard Norris), The White Horse (James Pye), and The Saracen's Head (Thomas Sephton), A more recent Saracen's Head landlord – Hughie Sharrock pioneered the Formby/Halsall bus service, later extending it to Ormskirk on Thursdays and Saturdays.

H. Blackhurst, Richard Cave, John Charles and Thomas Segar are shown as yeoman farmers. The professional (or unemployed!) are as follows:

Sir William Farley Bart. M.P. – Broadwood House;
John Higson (attorney);

Mr Thomas Higson;

The Rev. Richard Loxham is Rector and the Rev. George Holden, presumably, a curate;

William Price (veterinary surgeon);

Mr Henry Rigby and Mrs Elizabeth Swift – presumably people of leisure!

Miss J. Mawdesley and Thomas Sumner are teachers the latter being also parish clerk.

Miss Mawdesley has become James Mawdesley (49) by 1841 in the census returns now available for examination at Ormskirk Library. At the same time, Thomas Sumner is shown as James (aged 65). Perhaps some of the census taking was not particularly accurate! John Thompson and James Pendleton are shown as grocers; James Moorcroft is a butcher; possibly John Kirby has taken over from father Henry as the blacksmith. Thomas Blundell is also a blacksmith and Peter Wilson is the saddler. There are still plenty of wheelwrights – Harry Blundell in Old Lane and Richard Norris and John Blundell in New Street. Is it a sign of growing affluence that so many shoemakers appear on the scene? William Fairhust is in New Street and Richard Blundell, Thomas Moorcroft and John Gill in the village. James Park is a draper and Henry Winstanley is one of two tailors.

What is significant in these 1841 details is the emergence of a significant number of boat-people. Many Halsall residents are now involved with the life of the canal. Some – not surprisingly – live on Halsall Hill, others in Morris Lane and Altcar Lane. On census night, three folk were, in fact, sleeping on barges.

The 1851 returns remind us of the impressive number of farmers presumably renting parcels of land from the estate. Not all of these tenants were Halsall born. Thomas Charles, farming 32 acres at Northmoor, had been born in Ormskirk; John Langton, with 75 acres at 57 Croft Lane, was from Scarisbrick; Peter Higson farmed 64 acres at 74 Renacres Lane and hailed from Skelmersdale.

There was a significant meeting in July 1884 relating to farm labourers. This was a period when there was national anxiety about the level of drinking. There were cries in some quarters for 'temperance legislation'. In line with this, the Church of England Temperance Society had initiated a meeting in Halsall at which the Rector presided. The newspaper report[4] is headlined 'The use of Beer in the Hay and Harvest Field' and the Secretary of the Agricultural Branch of the Society spoke – for an hour – about the practice of giving beer to harvest workers as part wages. 'Did giving beer,' he asked, 'help towards the economical and successful in-gathering of the harvest?' 'It was,' he claimed, 'unfair to present temptation in the way of young men.' One farmer said there would be difficulties in

The village's very own band. The date and location are unknown.

changing long-term customs, but they were, doubtless, preaching to the converted. Farmers T. Mawdesley, J. Cropper, R. Norris, J. Marshall, J. Harrison, E. Banks, G. Weatherby – and someone referred to merely as Ambrose – unanimously passed the resolution, 'That, in the opinion of this conference, it is desirable in the interests of masters and men that the practice of giving beer in hay and harvest time be discontinued and that money payments or some other drink be supplied instead'. There is no record as to whether any change in the arrangement was made. In fairness, the drink problem was not confined just to the employed. A newspaper three years earlier[5] had reported that 37-year-old farmer James Hesketh of Halsall Moss had over-indulged himself at Liverpool Market and had died in a state of drunkenness. The inquest at the Blue Bell, Barton, had put his death down to 'natural causes'.

Farmers also sometimes had monetary problems. Newspaper reports in June and August 1879[6] give details of a court action Sumner v. Levi. Local farmer Mr Sumner, who had got heavily involved with Liverpool money-lenders, was complaining about damage when Mr Levi's agents had been removing assets under a bill of sale. Brighouse and Brighouse (a familiar name in the law locally) were acting for Mr Levi. Against a claim of £48, their representative (Mr Segar) won compensation made up as follows:

Horses – £5, Machine – £10, Pig – £5, Roller – £1 5s., Saddle 10s. and Rope 5s. Mr Levi had to pay costs.

There was enough business in the area for the Manchester and Liverpool District Bank[7] – later The District Bank – to have a sub-branch in Halsall. The minutes of Bank's Board meeting of 14 November 1907 read:

> Since the meeting of the board on the 26 September, two sub-branches have been opened under the management of Ormskirk Office, viz. at Halsall on Tuesdays and Fridays commencing the 11 October and at Scarisbrick (Bescar Lane) commencing on 2 November.

Until 1 November 1967 – as a prelude to the sad demise of so much local banking – clerks came out and used a front room in a Summerwood Lane house. Halsall, unlike Barton and Scarisbrick, was denied its own District Bank premises. Williams Deacons Bank – latterly absorbed by The Royal Bank of Scotland – had a part-time branch in New Street. They had a room in the house originally occupied by the mole catcher Mr Scambler. Opened on the first of January 1920 – well after their rival, they kept going until 30 October 1970.[8] Students of the history of banking will want to ask why two Manchester-based banks rather than the Liverpool-based Martins Bank sought to meet Halsall's financial needs.

Farmers also had disease to combat. A report in 1879[9] says that Thomas Twist of Grigg's Farm had an outbreak of foot and mouth disease. There are folk still alive who can remember reporting such outbreaks to the village policeman who lived in part of the building behind St Cuthbert's Hall which houses the post office.

As well the service trades, the community found work for other trades and professions. John Maugham had come from Manchester to be the local bobby; Margaret Bond was a charwoman; Mary Rimmer of Park House (67 Plex Lane) a

Outbreaks of foot and mouth disease had to be reported to the local constable. This is P.C. Sisme in the 1920s.

The old St Cuthbert's Hall.

nurse; Alice Berry of 67 Morris Lane was a dressmaker; and Peter Heyes (at Halsall Hall) a gamekeeper. The estate once employed as many as half a dozen such keepers. Charlie Whittle is still remembered as chief game-keeper, having his own cottage near Rain Bag Wood on the way to Ainsdale. Thomas Park, grocer at 21 New Street, combined this work in 1851 with that of parish clerk. Richard Norris is described as an ostler – an intersting description! The other spelling is 'hostler' and the work is that of a stableman particularly associated with an inn.

Halsall was important because of its position on the canal. Perhaps there was also inn trade because of the main road. Fred Snape's cycle shop moved with the times and got involved in the motor trade in premises still associated with this industry. Later, Bill Threlfall opened a garage at the corner with Gregory Lane.

The census also reveals the life style of mid-nineteenth-century clergy. Richard Leigh was Rector in 1851. His two sons and two daughters were cared for by a governess. There were nine servants: cook/housekeeper, laundry maid, two house maids, a kitchen maid, nurse, butler, coachman and labourer.

Only one handloom weaver is shown – John Miller. But we know that there are still weavers' houses and cottages near Weaver's Bridge in Morris Lane – a suggestion that there must have been a cottage industry either before the Mordaunts set up the Halsall House factory or in conjunction with it.

James Houghton of 65 Morris Lane appears to have the monopoly of brickmaking. 51 Crofts Lane provides lodgings for someone seemingly out of place in nineteenth-century Halsall – an office clerk! But perhaps this clerk was the herald of other unexpected Halsall residents. By 1891, the railway having been operating for four years, and it is not surprising to find one Joseph Bentham lodging at 1 Runnel Lane. He is a railway signalman coming from Westmorland – these early railway workers must have moved around as opportunities occurred. John Dandy of 38 Shirdley Hill is down as a railway platelayer, Henry Rimmer (45 Lamanda Lane) is a signalman and William Shaw, railway stationmaster, has come from Lostock to 9 Carr Moss Lane where he has Jonathan Dobson, signalman from Yorkshire, lodging with him. James Mayor, 40 Aspinall Lane, is a railway labourer from Burscough.

The 1871 census gives Richard Fazakerley of 75 Small Lane as the engine driver of a threshing machine and, twenty years later, we find Richard Fairclough (69 Morris Lane) shown as driver of a traction engine which was owned, it seems, by his neighbour at No. 68. Heatons at Four Lane Ends in Renacres Lane are still remembered as owners of threshing machines which toured farms at harvest time. A mill was available for grinding corn for livestock and poultry feed: corn, hay and straw – everything to do with animal feeding – were sold. After a take-over, the business was run down.

In 1891, Nathan Prescott of 11 Cross Lane and Edward Woodcock (23 Dickinson Lane) represent another new development – market gardening – and Joseph Scarisbrick of 57 Renacres Lane is listed as a carrot dealer. John Seambles (58 New Street) is the mole catcher. If he did his job effectively from the start, he could live the life of a gentleman afterwards!

Some local residents have managed to provide all-time references to themselves in the buildings they have provided. Two houses in Carr Moss Lane with 'R&MA' on the front are said to be associated with Richard and Mary Aspinwall, still remembered as residents of Green Kettle Farm.

In more recent times, *The Lancashire Village Book*[10] has identified local characters who are still remembered. John Harrison, of Mill House Farm was 'The Goose King', stocking up in the autumn for the Christmas Market using stubble left after the corn had been harvested to fatten up his stock. Expert craftsmen included Mr Cores and Mr Mellings (blacksmiths). Mr Wilson (the name has already been mentioned in this connection) was a saddler and Mr Knowles was a wheelwright. There were hamper makers once growing their materials locally. Nurse Bond was 'the local-doctor-cum-nurse-cum-midwife, being of particular benefit to those too poor to engage a fully fledged doctor. As midwife and 'layer out', she was said to 'bring 'em in and take 'em out'! Doctors remembered are Doctors Suffern, Heal and Pendlebury – the latter owning the first motor car ever seen in

A rather poor photograph of John Harrison, 'The Goose King'.

Halsall. Mrs Snape had a small shop in her front room opposite the church and there were also two sisters who ran the Cocoa Rooms in the same locality selling sweets, cigarettes and pop. As one sister was known to give more generous measures than the other, there was often a certain jockeying for position about being served!

The services offered by the shops were augmented – sometimes competed with – by travelling salesmen.[11] Bread was delivered by Southport bakers Coultons. They scrapped their motto 'The Loaf that stopped Mother Baking' when the local retort was 'Yes, it jolly well killed her!' Outrams Bread also came out from Southport. One of their drivers – Jack Cook – was also in demand as an amateur entertainer. Rimmer's Bread from Southport was thought to be a cut above the products of the larger firms and some shoppers preferred to patronise Hayes with a Southport shop in Chapel Street. Jack Lyon came from his grocers in Ormskirk at the corner of Halsall Lane and Southport Road. Mrs Rigby also travelled from Ormskirk; the Scotts came from Birkdale. A Birkdale butcher from Eastbourne Road and Biltcliffes from Ainsdale also thought it worthwhile to bring supplies to the village. Horse transport operated initially, to be replaced gradually by motor vans.

A horse and cart is still associated with coalman Harry Blundell, known locally as 'Sugar' His brother accompanied him rocking backwards and forwards as the wagon went through the village. 'Sugar' was replaced on his death by 'Slack' – Jim Fairclough. There was a big demand for paraffin – a vital commodity in the days before electricity – and soap, candles, lamps, lamp glasses, wicks, matches and crockery were also brought out. 'Guzunders' were available – much in demand prior to indoor sanitation! Fruiterer Sheridan's rich plum-like voice shouted out the list of what was currently available. Operating from Burscough Street, Ormskirk, the busi-

Above: Halsall Mothers' Union in the 1950s.

Below: Winners of the Best Kept Village award, early 1950s.

A day out for the Halsall Conservative ladies.

ness passed to Stan Huyton and there was enough work for brother Harry to operate an alternative round within the village. Stan's reputation for being late with his deliveries was put down to his attraction to the local hostelries! It was alleged that his horse automatically pulled up outside every pub en route!

Sheridan, Greengrocer/Fruiterer, was a regular visitor with his sales cry, 'Apples, oranges, onions, bananas, tomatoes, lemons, plums-ripe'. Not surprisingly, he was known as 'Plum-Ripe'!

There was a travelling tailor to measure you for a suit. Mr Waiting came from his Aughton Street shop where Safeways is now. His slogan – 'My wares wear where wear is wanted!' If your need was for nails, screws, staples etc., there was yet another Ormskirk trader – 'Staple-Nail Lizzie' – who often slept overnight in a local barn. Every Sunday, a newsagent walked from Ormskirk to provide the Sunday papers – lunchtime, no doubt, before getting down to the latest revelations in *The News of the*

World. Summer Sundays were also the occasion for a visit from a Birkdale Fernley Road horse-drawn ice cream vendor. The stock was soon sold on a very hot day!

Wheeler-dealer Davy Brookfield would be able to sell you anything. This week it might be fish but, much as you might like your purchase, there was no guarantee a similar product would be available next week! But, whatever your needs, you only needed to ask and Davy and diddy assistant Jack, with even more mysterious sources of supply, could oblige.

Many of the big houses in the village had large gardens and hardworking tenants claimed to be able to raise enough for their rents by what they could grow. 'Hucksters' such as Jimmy Houghton and Jack Stopforth with their Ford wagons were prepared to collect produce and, for a small commission, sell it at Liverpool market. Halsall Hall Farm opposite the school was very much associated with Dick Cropper and his son.

The village has always participated in the Southport and District Football League. Matches played originally on the field behind the church were known locally by the name of the current captain – Ashy's Team, when Henry Ashcroft was in charge, became Socket's Team when Harry left the district. The field on which the matches were played was well equipped with running tracks etc., and Halsall was venue for competitions well attended by competitors from other areas.

Like most villages, Halsall is now without shops and most of the travelling salesmen have disappeared. Their place has been taken by a free bus provided by Tesco's Southport. Starting in Haskayne on Tuesdays and Fridays, the bus reaches Halsall Church at 9.41 a.m. Shoppers get fifty minutes in the store before being returned home.[12] Better than nothing for those without their own transport, but a far cry from the days when shopping facilities were much more local!

CHAPTER EIGHT

The Masses Against the Classes[1]

The village for the villagers.[2]

I N AUGUST 1897, *The Ormskirk Advertiser*[3] drew attention to a newly published Royal Commission report on 'Agricultural Depression'. The *Advertiser* complained about the depopulation of the countryside; younger and more enterprising members of rural communities were leaving for the towns where wages were higher and there was more constant employment. Even the modest village industries which had previously helped country folk to eke out a living had been absorbed into the towns. 'Life in these quiet out-of-the-way places', said the paper, 'is of a very torpid nature. Village life has not received the attention from politicians and economist which it deserves'.

It was presumably Gladstone's wish not to be tarred with the same brush as 'politicians and economists' of this sort that prompted him to bring an exhausted parliament back into session in November, and drive them through the Christmas period to get The Local Government (or Parish Council) legislation on to the statute book.[4] In was Liverpool seven years earlier that he had said that 'All the world over, I will back the masses against the classes'[5], and this legislation is said to have been the major achievement of his 1892–4 period as Prime Minister.[6]

The main hope was that the creation of parish councils would give 'an opportunity to encourage the political consciousness of rural workers'.[7] The Scarisbrick meeting was on 1 January 1895, but Halsall beat Scarisbrick by nearly two weeks in getting its first meeting off the ground. However, unlike Ainsdale, Tarleton, Banks, Bickerstaffe Lathom/Burscough and Aughton, neither Scarisbrick nor Halsall seem to have courted press coverage. This was in stark contrast to Formby, which hogged many column-inches in announcing what it was going to do – or not do![8]

At the time the new council was set up, Charles Arnold Baker's[9] description of English parish councils probably fitted late 19th-century Halsall like a glove:

'In 1894 the squire, the parson and sometimes the schoolmaster were the leaders of the village. Their influence depended upon their prestige, superior education, relative wealth and social standing. The vestries had followed their lead. The parish councils were regarded as an intrusion. Most of them began without the co-operation of the influential. Worse still, agriculture had entered upon the long decline which only ended with the Second World War. The revenues of parish councils came mainly from rates on agricultural land, which in 1895 was derated by fifty per cent'.

The idea was that rural workers should put themselves up for election to the new body, but it would have taken a very bold tenant in Halsall to be involved in what might be construed as a 'village revolution'. Here was a council of 'civil origin, status and affiliation'. 'As a result', says Baker, 'the church was excluded from formal participation in local government and the traditional functions of the parish, which had always had a 'Christian' complexion, were to be administered by laymen'. Admittedly, 800 amendments were tabled as the bill had gone through parliament and the opposition had ensured that spending should be limited to the equivalent of a threepenny rate, but married women – as well as spinsters – could now vote in local elections. No wonder, as Baker says, all 'this caused perturbation'.

We can imagine that such 'perturbation' was no more evident than in Halsall. Those with family connections with the membership of Halsall's very first Parish Council will be able to tell us about the background of these village councillors. Were any of them farm labourers? Were some of them artisans and local tradesmen? Were there any who felt confident enough to 'rock the boat'? There is certainly no indication from the minutes of the early meetings that anyone wanted 'to take on the Establishment'.[10]

This glancing blow at democracy got underway at a parish meeting held in the schoolroom on 4 December 1894. Even though Mr Gladstone resigned in March over the question of Irish Home Rule, there was still a Liberal government in power. The Manchester Ship Canal had been opened in January and Tower Bridge in June. Aviator Sir Alan Cobham had been born in May and J. B. Priestley in September; Robert Louis Stevenson had died the day before the meeting. The wealthier members of the Halsall community would still be smarting from the introduction, in August, of Death Duties, and Marks and Spencer had opened their first Penny Bazaar at Cheethem Hill, Manchester, on 30 September.

But we still had not got round to having women at public meetings. Those present at the meeting to elect members to the new Parish Council were:

Job Grimshaw, Edward Threlfall, James Marshall, Thomas Ball, Samuel

Park, James Moorcroft, Joseph Harrison, Edward Culshaw, Thomas Howard, John Rimmer, Thomas Prescott, Robert Rimmer, R. Mawdesley and Job Bradshaw.

Surprise, surprise! The Rector, Canon Blundell, was unanimously appointed as Chairman. The 'village revolution' had not arrived!

The Councillors resulting from this election procedure were:

R. Aspinwall – Plumpton Lane
T. Ball – New Cut Lane
E. Culshaw – Plex Lane
J. Grimshaw – Renacre Lane
J. Harrison – Carr Moss Lane
J. Moorcroft – Dickenson Lane
E. Threlfall – Narrow Lane

At subsequent parish meetings, appointments were made of Tax Assessors, Waywarden etc., and the accounts of charities and amounts for voluntary rates were approved. As the years go by, parish meetings appear to get more spasmodic and the length of the minutes shorter. One of the problems may be that no one was very sure about the minute book in which to record proceedings. There is, however, a breakthrough in March 1931.

The meeting, say the minutes, presented a new feature 'with the presence of ladies'. 'It was understood', said the clerk, 'that they were anxious to know when the parish might expect Electricity.' An official who was present gave an assurance that power would be available before the end of the current year. There was also a complaint about the disposal of house refuse, and a decision to allocate four more council houses to Halsall. In 1934, residents of New Cut Lane were still awaiting their supply, even though the wiring had been in place for two years, and ash bins were still being emptied irregularly. A plea was made that there should be a better attendance at the lectures that had been arranged on Agriculture.

But there were no ladies at the first meeting of the Parish Council on 19 December 1894. Those present were:

Messrs. Aspinwall, Ball, Culshaw, Grimshaw, Harrison, Moorcroft and Threlfall. Again, Canon Blundell was unanimously chosen as Chairman – still no desire here to topple the Church from its traditional role! Mr Mawdesley was appointed Temporary Clerk at a salary of £2 per annum. Mr R. Shaw became Treasurer, and Williams Deacons Bank, now part of the Royal Bank of Scotland, were subsequently appointed bankers.

The present Parish Council is in process of lodging the Council's minutes in the Lancashire Record Office in Preston and they will be available for all to read. If nothing else, these valuable records are a reminder that our standard of handwriting is not what it used to be! The copper-plate style of the early minutes eventually gave way to a scroll which is not always easy to read. We must be grateful for word processors which make modern-day minute keeping so much easier to undertake – and to read!

A painstaking and detailed examination of the older minutes would obviously give a very good 'grass roots' picture of Halsall life over the last century, but all that is possible at this stage is to pick out one or two items which catch the eye after an hour or two's examination of the documents. A change in the nature of the work done by the Council over the years is immediately apparent. At that first meeting Messrs. Threlfall, Grimshaw and Aspinwall were appointed to collect rents and distribute dole on St John's Day 1894. The purchase of Dole Bread for the period Easter to 13 December 1894 amounted to £3 15s.

One of the Council's first tasks was to place a stone in the wall to the right of the lych gate to commemorate the 60th anniversary of Victoria's reign. The 1897 list shown on the stone suggests that Cllrs Ball and Harrison had been replaced. The list, still available for all to see, reads:

The Parish Council of Halsall 1997 –

Job Grimshaw
Edward Culshaw
Thomas Howard
Richard Aspinwall
Edward Threlfall
Edward Banks
James Moorcroft.

Of the Queen, the Council says: 'Whom God preserve. She wrought her people lasting good.'

Similarly, the Coronation of George V on 24 June 1911 is celebrated on another stone opposite the church next to the bus shelter. An oak tree was planted behind it by Mrs Blundell and Mrs Scarlon – an aged Halsall resident.[11]

Problems with flooding occupy members' time at regular intervals. In July 1928, the state of the drainage at the West End of Morris Lane is reported. In July 1932, there had been flooding in front of the Shirdley Hill Post Office. In August 1942, there had been flooding to a depth of several inches in Segars Lane. The land near the lane was also flooded in March 1944 because Sandy Brook had overflowed, and there was flooding near the church in April 1946.

On 15 April 1895, it was agreed to ask Southport Water Works – presumably at their Scarisbrick site – if their water mains could be used in case of fire. In October of the same year, it was agreed to ask neighbouring councils to join Halsall in maintaining the steam fire engine stationed in Ormskirk.

Getting in and out of the village was another regular concern of parish councillors. At the first meeting, they agreed to enquire about the availability of salt for roads in frosty weather. The April 1907 meeting called for traffic danger signs on certain roads – obviously the motor car was beginning to have an impact on village life. Ribble Motors were constantly approached about bus services. In June 1934, a member complained about disparities between railway fares on the local line. Shirdley Hill–Southport was 3 pence single; Halsall–Southport was 8 pence, so something was clearly wrong here! On 16 June 1938, the Council complained about the withdrawal of passenger services on the Downholland branch line. Despite wartime fuel rationing, there was a call to Ribble Motors in August 1943 for more buses to Southport for shoppers. In common with most parish councils, Halsall has always given attention to the provision of bus shelters.

The state of 'their' roads is always a good topic for local councils, and Halsall councillors kept Lancashire County Council on its toes. A discussion at the March 1936 meeting – the Choir Vestry seems to have been the

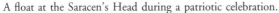

A float at the Saracen's Head during a patriotic celebration.

usual venue at this time – is a reminder of an era which has passed. The County Council were urged to reconstruct the section of Segars Lane from Barn House Farm to White Otter Farm, as the surface was suffering because of the heavy summer traffic to Ainsdale Lido, which is sadly no more! In August 1939, there were complaints about the conduct of campers in the Segars Lane area. In more recent times (October 1974) alarm was expressed at the number of heavy container lorries using minor lanes.

During the two wars, the minutes do not refer as much as might be expected to problems which must have arisen. A 3 pm meeting on 6 November 1943 – very badly attended – is an indication that the 'black-out' was restricting evening activities. Efforts to encourage villagers to lighten the long, dark evenings with a good book had come to nothing. The Ormskirk Librarian complained to the August 1942 meeting that there was a significant lack of interest in books provided for Halsall. The problem seemed to be that no key to the 'library' was available on a Saturday afternoon when the librarian came to the village!

There was an interesting request from the Leeds and Liverpool Canal authorities for volunteers to construct what seem to be described as 'stops' on the canal near Halsall Bridge to be used in the event of air raids. Whether or not these were some sort of shelter is unclear. The Council did not seem to know who would use them. The concensus seems to have been 'If the canal wants 'em, they can build 'em themselves!'

More constructively, money was given in November 1943 to the Halsall Platoon of the Home Guard. Every effort was made to encourage the salvage of waste paper, iron and rags. The February 1943 meeting – and others – shows a very clear commitment to the 'Wings for Victory' campaign. The plight of areas less fortunate than Halsall is highlighted by a request from West Lancashire Rural District Council that 8 volunteers be recruited to make a house-to-house collection, on 19 August 1941, for 'The Air Raid Distress Fund'.

Just before the war, in May 1938, there had been a request from farm labourers for adequate accommodation. An acute shortage of housing at a reasonable rent existed and Rector Mather was on a District Council committee looking into the problem. He had made representations for 20 houses and was asked to appeal from the pulpit about any likely take-up of accommodation made available. But interest in local housing had been on hold during the war. When it ended, there was, as expected, a real drive to provide additional housing accommodation for returning service men and women. On 30 May 1944, a special Parish Meeting was called to discuss the proposal to build 64 houses on Carr Moss Lane. Those taking part in the discussion agreed that more accommodation was required but they accused the rural district council of keeping the village in the dark. It was felt that 64 houses in one place would 'react on the present residents in the area involved'. 'Rural slums' could arise; the houses were for agricultural workers and should be nearer their work.

A list of alternative sites for a smaller number of houses in each case was given. The following areas were mentioned: Plex Moss Lane, Plex Lane

Lady Lethbridge (née Hilda Blundell) was very much involved in local affairs. She is seen here with her husband, Major Lethbridge.

St Cuthbert's Hall was once used by local thespians. *Top*: A Viennese evening in the 1950s. *Bottom*: Halsall Dramatic Club, 1949.

near the canal, Carr Moss Lane, Summerwood Lane, Bangors Green, Gregory Lane, Northmoor Lane (again near the canal), Weavers House Bridge, Shirdley Hill and Mill House Farm.

The Council stated that 32 houses in the parish which had been condemned should be replaced. Lady Lethbridge – whose involvement in parish affairs was very marked at this period – urged residents to move with the times. The resolution accepted was that 32 houses should be built on the sites suggested, as a concentration of 64 on one site was not acceptable. In July 1946, the Council was told that 46 new houses had been sanctioned against an application for 39.

From time to time, the Parish Council delved into the mysteries of ownership of some of the village's older buildings. In November 1947, it grappled with the problem of the appointment of trustees for the Halsall Cocoa Rooms. The Church of England Temperance Society – or 'The Tontine Club', as the clerk put in brackets – and Lady Lethbridge seem to have had some involvement. In May 1955, questions were asked about the ownership of the Hearse House and, in October 1975, what to do with a disused telephone exchange was also on the agenda. Asked, in October of the previous year, about local buildings of architectural interest, 28 Renacres Lane, La Mancha Hall, 'Courtyard of No. 2' (?) and Halsall Hall were put forward as likely candidates.

The Rector was present at the September 1953 meeting to ask the Council to consider taking over responsibility for the St Cuthbert's Hall. Members, however, preferred the idea of a new building on the playing fields. More recent meetings have involved a considerable amount of business relating to the playing field complex. Members have always seemed very proud of their rotary mower, if the frequency with which it appears in their minutes is anything to go by! July 1962 saw the earth-shattering decision to ban coconuts from Rose Queen ceremonies! In recent times, there has been the unfortunate theft of the playing field ornamental gates and some confusion about their replacement.

It is not surprising that, with all this attention, Halsall Playing Fields have, at least once, been awarded the certificate for the Best Kept Playing Field. Representatives of the Council went to Blackpool in 1961 to receive the award. The village has also been the winner of the Best Kept Village Competition organised by the Community Council of Lancashire. This distinction was obtained in 1977 and there will probably be long-standing residents who will tell us that this was not the only time that Halsall swept the board. At the meeting in February 1978, the village was asked to give someone else a chance and not to enter for the 1978 competition. The 'Certificate of Merit for the Best Kept Churchyard' was received in September 1964. No doubt there have also been more recent awards of this sort.

Halsall Parish Council has traditionally had close links with its village school and a place on the school's board of governors is available to them.

At the January 1937 meeting, there was an item from Cllr J. Harrison – a school manager – which would bring present-day equal opportunities champions to screaming pitch. The then Lancashire Education Committee had ruled that, on marriage, all female teachers should resign! The Halsall managers were, apparently, not opposing the general principle. But, 'cap in hand', although they would, from now on, demand resignation from new appointments who embraced matrimony, they were seeking special dispensation for those married ladies currently teaching at Halsall Central School.

There was a reminder in June 1932 that Halsall is an agricultural community at a meeting that Halsall Council had convened with their Downholland neighbours, when plans of action in relation to various rural pests were discussed. The government had introduced legislation making each farmer responsible for dealing with their own rats and mice. The opportunity was taken at the meeting to highlight the problem of moles 'pressing further into the parish at various points'! The Scarisbrick, Halsall and Downholland Estate was criticised for abolishing the Mole Rate, which, although it was only a few shillings a year, had paid for the services of a mole catcher. It was agreed to make representations to the Estate about the problem.

The Bishop's Walk.

In more recent times, the Parish Council, one of more than 7,000 nationally, that has taken on the role set out in modern legislation. Surprisingly, 26,400 people work for such councils – one third of them on a voluntary basis. Members make comments about local planning applications, keep footpaths and can, in some areas, be involved with allotments, arts, recreation, burials, public clocks and war memorials.

Notably, in the recent past, Halsall Council has worked with the District Council in providing an attractive nature walk to the right of what was once the Scarisbrick Arms. Members have been involved in an enhancement scheme for the cross near the church lych gate and there has been dialogue with the District Council about a proposal for a roundabout in this area. There has also been an involvement in the District Council's Stone Wall Repair Scheme in the village's conservation area. Additionally, in an effort to reduce the drift from the village by young people, there have been proposals, as at other times, to increase the amount of local low cost housing. There was a spirited campaign opposing plans for establishing a unit producing compost which would, it was alleged, give off odours detrimental to the country area.

Parish Councillors in 2000 are:

Gerard Riley (Chairman)
Philip Howell (Vice-Chairman)
Dave Corfield
Raymond Brookfield
Peter Lea
Alan Webster
Doreen Stephenson.
Elaine Woodhead (Clerk)

The Council is different in two ways from that which met for the first time in December 1894. The ladies have now – quite rightly – got in on the act, and the different climate from that existing a century ago has made it possible for local members to be more immediately in touch with their political colleagues at national, district and county level. Far more than in 1894, Parish Councils give 'an opportunity to encourage the political consciousness of rural workers', [12] as well as representing the needs of those who, thanks to improved transport, can choose to live in a village like Halsall.

CHAPTER NINE

Built and Endowed [1]

The Churches have claim before history to a continued honourable role in English Education. [2]

'**E**DWARD'S LOVE OF LEARNING induced him to found numerous grammar schools which bore his name' [3] – a statement generally made about Edward VI but which, in Halsall's case, applies to school-founder Edward Halsall. Although Edward VI reigned for only six years (1547–1553), the Boy King must have been very busy as an educationist, as there are many schools up and down the country claiming him as their founder. His namesake in Halsall must have been inspired by what was happening elsewhere; the village was only forty years behind in establishing their church school in 1593. 'The Reformation and the fear and hatred of Spain felt in the second half of the sixteenth century', says Peter Cousins, [4] 'did not in any way lessen Christian concern for education'.

Halsall was even ahead of Ormskirk and Liverpool; Henry Ascroft founded their grammar school in 1610 and the Liverpool Bluecoat School was not built until 1726. Baines [5] is said to have confused the grammar schools of North Meols and Halsall, but the former was not apparently founded until 1700 [6] – very much later than Halsall. We have already seen that Nathaniel Brownell – Rector a century later – had a faculty for teaching boys. According to Baines, [7] there were 54 boys on roll in September 1827, with a greater number in the winter. The Master's wife kept a school for girls in the upper room. Finance came from the parents according to their means.

In 1861, the school was moved to a former tithe barn adjoining the graveyard on a site fronting Summerwood Lane on the bend near the church. Log books starting on 27 July 1863 [8] show 54 boys on roll. The main aim all the time is to try to get registered pupils into school and community activities do not make this easy. With the passing of the 1870 Education Act, Education should have been taken more seriously but, as with most areas, Halsall was, apparently, slow in entering into the spirit of the new legislation. 'This has been a broken week. The school was

As local people will clearly remember, during the early part of the last century the school made a special point of teaching practical skills. The photographs on these pages illustrate the education of husbandry, domestic science, woodwork, etc.

required for parochial purposes', says an entry on 14 February 1896. Poor attendance is recorded because of the Anniversary of the Village Cup, and later the same year, there are holidays on 11 September 1896 because of the Annual Tea Party, and another break three weeks later – the building is needed for an entertainment. Within a fortnight, there are three more days off – Monday is the Temperance Ball, Thursday Confirmation and Friday the Scholars' Tea Party, hosted by Count de Casteja.

Above: A 1930s' view of the school buildings.

Below: Pressure of increasing numbers led to the construction of additional accommodation, built in the 1950s and 1960s.

The turn of the century sees complete re-organisation: co-education arrives! Reactions to the changes are evident in the school's log book: '21 December 1899 – The first half-year's work as a mixed school brought to a close. The Upper Standards like the change', and 'Girls are evidently benefiting by the change'. Baines tells us that an enquiry into Education in Halsall was held in March 1901. It revealed that the schoolmaster was appointed by the Select Vestry at the request of the then Lord of the Manor, Thomas Scarisbrick, who was in fact a Roman Catholic. The schoolmaster received an annuity each year of £13 6s. 8d. (£13.33). Twelve boys of the parish and township of Halsall and Downholland were taught free, and 'As many other poor children of those townships as apply are admitted at a reduced rate of quarterage according to the rate fixed by the vestry at the time of the master's appointment'. By September 1902, the average attendance for the half year is 201, compared with 176 for the corresponding period in the previous year.

The tablet on the exterior of the present building says:

> Canon B. H. Blundell, Rector of Halsall, and Colonel B. H. Blundell CB late Grenadier Guards built these Church of England Schools for the benefit of the children of Halsall AD 1904. 'In the lips of him who has understanding wisdom is found'.

But the school log suggests that full occupation of the new building was not achieved until the beginning of 1907. The 7 January 1907 entry reads: 'The scholars assembled in the old school at 9 am. this morning. Books and stationery were given out and the scholars prepared for marching to the New Schools'. The buildings were, appropriately, in New Street – now part of the A5147.

A month later, we have an HMI report. 'The children are now housed', it says, under 'new and beautiful conditions. Having regard to the good work that was done in the old premises, a hope may now be expressed that intelling [sic] training suitable as a training for rural life may distinguish the future of the school in the highest degree'. Comments such as these, along with the introduction in April 1907 of gardening for 14 top boys each Wednesday afternoon, and followed shortly afterwards by cookery for the older girls, suggest that it was not thought that pupils would venture very far from the village in adult life. The gardening sessions offered very relevant 'hands-on' experience. On 9 January 1915, in the middle of World War I, the weather was 'adverse' so gardening activities included:

1. Trimming and making labels for the coming season.

2. Setting up potatoes for seed.

3. Sorting various seeds saved from last season.

There was a special cookery lesson for the girls when, on 23 March 1938 they were involved in poultry dressing and trussing and preparing an exhibit for the Royal Lancashire Show – the last before World War II.

And all the time there are the well-defined links with the community. '13 May 1907 – School closed earlier as children coming back early for homecoming of Mr & Mrs Blundell of Halsall House – 2 school managers'. Nearly a century before scholars had been 'invited to Scarisbrick Hall to share in the festivities connected with the return home of the Count's son with his Bride from their honeymoon'. As well as acknowledging the local gentry, the children were also well-schooled in matters of patrotism: '24 May 1907 – In accordance with the instructions from the Lancashire Education Committee, today was observed as Empire Day'.

Attendance was also affected by several other factors. There were the inevitable children's diseases and in July 1907 school was closed for eight weeks because of scarlet fever. The realities of life in a rural village meant that boys were kept off regularly to help in the fields: '2nd October 1871 – Many boys are still absent. This is owing to the unnaturally long harvest'. 'Several boys in the upper standards have been away this week,' says the 8 March 1878 entry, 'Field work is about to commence'. There is an 1886 reference to what is now called an Education Welfare Officer – the old 'School Board' – but presumably his influence was not very great! He would probably have been part-time, combining the work with that of a poor law relieving officer, or even a local shopkeeper. It would have meant a £2 a year increase on his normal salary – hardly a big incentive to chase

The potato harvest involved the whole family. This is the Heaton family in the 1950s.

children back into school. In any case, even if parents were prosecuted, the fine would be in the region of 2*s*. 6*d*. (12½ pence) [9]

Things did not improve in the new century: '1902 October 20 – School opened this morning with 75 children absent. The morning was wet but many children are still employed in the potato fields where they can earn 12 shillings per week'. In October 1907, they read in the press that the Ormskirk District Education Committee had decided not to take proceedings against boys staying away from school 'for such a good reason'. By 1909, they have established an October 'Potato Harvest Holiday'.

And even 'when all had been safely gathered in', there was still the weather! 'It would have been far better to have closed the school during the whole week', says an exasperated headteacher on 16 February 1900. 'The weather has been so wintery that there scarcely have been any scholars'.

Two 'School-Board' officers are still remembered. Officer Blundell was easy-going and rarely visited unless a pupil was absent for a long time. His successor, Officer Cunliffe, soon altered all this and parents and children were, in the words of one of the children in his care, 'scared stiff of him'. 'No-one took any liberties with Cunliffe. He was nicknamed 'The Comforter' (Lord knows why! Perhaps the inventer of the nickname had in mind the Bayeux Tapestry, one of whose panels shows the King goading on his soldiers with a spear in their backsides. The caption reads 'The King Comforteth his troops'!)

But even if you can get them into school, can you teach them? The entry for 8 September 1899 shows great despondency:

> Commenced work on Monday after a holiday of 4 weeks beyond the usual time. This is owing to the impossibility of obtaining two qualified assistants for the school, which is worked as a mixed and infants school. Many applicants came to see the school. They all appeared to be satisfied with the school and its surroundings but, on their return to their friends, all declined to accept the situation. Probably the school house and being so far from town are the chief causes of refusal.

It is not surprising that 1899 is recorded as showing the most 'distastrous half year ever experienced' because of 'problems with staff recruitment', and failure to obtain assistance in 1900 necessitated the extension of the Autumn holiday by a further two weeks.

Because of the pre-occupation with attendance and standards, the log books are not as full of anecdotes as they are in some schools, but the entry for 19 October 1909 is an exception. It reads:

> 19 October 1909 – Owing to children spending money sometimes too freely a rule has been made that no child must go to the sweet shop without

Links between church and school have always been close in Halsall.

permission. Today, a boy went without that permission and was served a shilling's worth of Bengal Lights. On cross examination, he admitted stealing the shilling from home. I sent a note to his mother and the only result is that she is keeping him at home as a punishment!

In June 1912 the Bishop visits. 'He expressed himself as most delighted and considered we had the best equipped rural school in his diocese', says the Head. This is not a surprising statement; there would not have been a lot of primary schools in the Liverpool area able to muster the resources available to Halsall. But despite improved conditions, the problems of getting 'bottoms on seats' still caused problems with standards:

14 June 1873 – Boys in Standard III are backward in all subjects. Most of them attend irregularly at school.

8 March 1878 – It is the irregular boys who keep the others back.

17 April 1896 – Boys in Standard IV are dull and want careful watching.

County Hall records [10] state that central heating was installed in 1935, but some of those who had attended the school claim that there was a boiler before that date. Arthur Mawdesley was caretaker, and when coke

Above: A popular school caretaker, Eric Kenyon, retires.

Below: A prize-giving ceremony. Graham Midgley and Mrs Midgley with headteacher Mr Doug Bonner.

was delivered he gave an impressive display of strength as he put the fuel down the manhole into the cellar.

Before the full implementation of the secondary school provisions of the 1944 Education Act which, in some areas, were not realised until the 1960s, Halsall was designated as a Central School. This afforded curriculum

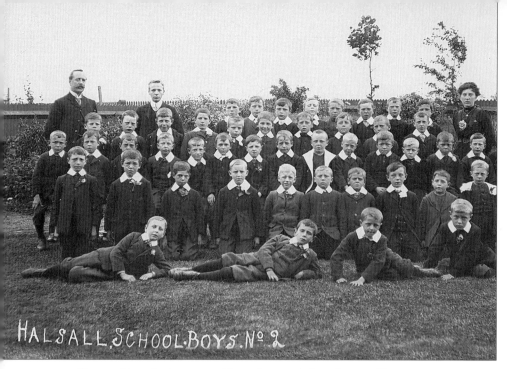

How would a school manage without the annual class photograph?

Princess Diana receives an enthusiastic reception during a local visit.

opportunities which, although by no means as elaborate as those of a grammar school, were a little better than the average all-age school in which chidren stayed for the whole of their school careers. This meant that chidren travelled into the village from areas like Scarisbrick and Haskayne.

In June 1929 the newly appointed Headteacher, A. H. Battersby, demonstrated the current policy of marketing your school with remarkable skill. He was described – or described himself – as a 'live wire', combining 'energy and ability with wide vision'. He had previously been an assistant master at All Saints, Wennington Road, Southport and had been Head of Saddleworth Parochial School.

A very good spread in *The Ormskirk Advertiser*[11] claimed that Halsall was 'one of the best equipped schools in the district'. 'It lends itself admirably', said the report, 'to the purpose of a central school.' The late Canon Blundell had built a school that was 'ahead of the times in layout and scheme', and which conformed 'closely to modern ideals'. With 230 pupils on the roll, 60 had been transferred to the central department from Scarisbrick and Haskayne and they were transported to and from school by 'motor bus', operated by Hughie Sharrock and paid for, it was believed, by Lady Lethbridge – the former Miss Blundell. There was ample room if the school-leaving age (then 14) should be raised. There were four school 'houses' – Hereward, Drake, Nelson and Segrave. There was keen competition to fulfil the school motto 'Work and Win'.

A large dining room is remembered as a distinctive feature of the building, but originally there were no meals provided. Children could, however, take

Photographs of staff and pupils from half a century ago.

pies and other food to be warmed up and it was possible to get an egg boiled. Mrs Whalley was in charge and she made tea for pupils. There was plenty of accommodation with tables and benches. Children living near the school went home.

By the time Mr Battersby arrived, the catering was more sophisticated. A threepenny school meal ranging from hot pot to fish pie and sausage to beef steak pudding was augmented by an 'abundant supply of bread'. There was fruit every day and Horlicks every morning.

The school garden and the cookery instruction for girls were mentioned. The infants department with its impressive painting of Lady Lethbridge

(Hilda Blundell) had recently received the handsome gift of a gramophone from Mrs Cope of Halsall House. New cycle sheds were provided in 1954 for the staggering cost of £54!

Because of the special status, there were as many as 200 on roll in 1952. A large staff house – once accommodating the Head and part of which was available for overnight use by assistant teachers – was brought into use for the teaching of Housecraft. A playshed/garage was made into a classroom in 1953. Sanitation was upgraded, in 1954, to Elsan chemical closets. Lord Derby opened a new assembly hall in 1955. There were further improvements to sanitation in 1965 and 1974. Under the legislation, Halsall assumed 'voluntary aided status' in 1951. With the full working out of 'secondary education for all', 11 plus children ultimately travelled to schools in Ormskirk and Southport for schooling up to the age of 15 and then 16.

Older residents remember Headteacher George Battersby as a strict disciplinarian. No doubt he had to sort out problems created by Miss Quine, whose frailty was taken advantage of by her pupils. Miss Meadowcroft and Miss Halsall came in by train from Southport and Miss Manson walked from Ormskirk on Monday mornings, returning home on Friday evenings! Miss Quine and Miss Hill had accommodation in the School House. These were the days when lady teachers contemplating matrimony had to resign!

When the *Southport Visiter* did a feature on the village in October 1979,[12] there were 100 children on roll from an area including Shirdley Hill, Barton, Haskayne and as far away as the Clieves Hills. 'Apart from school activities,' says the report, 'the school is "home" to a playgroup five mornings a week and has a very important evening role to play in village life.' In addition to uniformed organisations, there is a youth club – 'bursting at the seams' – and badminton classes. There is a week-end demand for use for wedding receptions and twenty-first birthday celebrations.

Currently, there are still 100 on roll and pupils are possibly drawn from an even wider area than before. The opening, in 1999, of a special area for parish use has eased the strain on accommodation. Like all schools, St Cuthbert's now has to keep a careful eye on its budget which, in modern circumstances, is significantly higher and more sophisticated than the estimated expenditure recorded in the log book on 18 November 1907 for the year commencing 31 March 1908:

Fuel and Light – £70
Furniture Repairs – £2 13s.
Books, Stationery – £372 6s.
Wear and Tear on Premises – Nil.

CHAPTER TEN

The First Crack of the Whip!

Restore human legs as a means of travel. Pedestrians rely on food for fuel and need no special parking facilities. [1]

A CCESS TO THE PARISH is via the A567 and some minor roads. As most of civilisation followed the main, Warrington–Preston road, there was little demand to open up West Lancashire. Writers in 1897 [2] suggest, however, that there had been recent improvements in roads possibly because of the growth of Liverpool to Southport traffic. Indeed, a local resident born in 1914 and a pupil of Halsall School reports that the road surface outside the present-day playing fields was so good that it was a favourite place for playing with whips and tops rushing back to school as soon as the bell rang! Not a lot of traffic, perhaps, but reasonable facilities for it when it came!

'[There is] a significant number of roads of all classes in this landscape', says a current West Lancashire document.[3] Sadly, in common with other Lancashire villages and because of the development of larger agricultural units in response to demands from Europe, these roads are having to cater for much larger vehicles than were ever intended for them. Ironically, over the years, Halsall has made two attempts to deal with the problem of moving large loads and both of them have 'had their day'. With the benefit of hindsight they may well have been kept in use rather than surrender the monopoly to the roads.

We have already seen that Halsall made a significant contribution to the Industrial Revolution manufacturing techniques. The same enterprise arose with the Leeds and Liverpool Canal. It was on Halsall Hill, near the Saracen's Head, on 5 November 1770 that the first sod was cut for the western section of the canal. The actual site was 400 yards beyond Bridge 24. Who better to use the spade than the enterprising Hon. Charles Mordaunt? The Act of Parliamant to allow construction was not passed until ten years later.

Halsall was on a busy thoroughfare between Liverpool Docks and the towns and villages of the North West. Of Halsall, the 1907 *Victoria County*

The first sod for the Leeds and Liverpool Canal's western section was cut near the Saracen's Head 230 years ago.

History[4] says, 'The Leeds and Liverpool Canal crosses the south-eastern portion of the township with the usual accompaniment of sett-laid roads and untidy wharfs.' An 1897 report[5] talks of 'rough country roads paved with huge cobble stones'. Peter Fleetwood-Hesketh[6] writes colourfully about the canal 'crossed at intervals by the deep stone bridges that are one of its most characteristic features, and seen here in a long diminishing perspective, the semi-ellipses of their whitened arches completed by reflection in the water. Sett-paved lanes [he says] wander eastward in the direction of Ormskirk.'

The canal was not used for distributing supplies to farms and getting goods to market. Traffic was more regional than local; The Wigan Coal & Iron Company is remembered particularly as having their own distinctively-marked barges. The main drawback to more local traffic was the remoteness of the wharf from the mossland. The failure of the attempt in the area of The Runnell to dig out a canal branch out towards Ainsdale and Birkdale, meant that farm supplies had still to be shifted by horse-drawn carts – a task usually undertaken in winter months when farm work was restricted.

A very significant passenger service also developed. 'Traffic was very slow', says Peter Aughton,[7] 'with horses lumbering along at a pedestrian pace and by the time the canal had meandered around the contours and climbed through the lock gates it was quicker to walk, but the ride was cheap and smooth and it was very convenient for people with heavy baggage to be carried.' Trips were advertised in 1790[8] 'with Maghull, Halsall, Burscough, Appley Bridge and Wigan as stopping places. The front cabin was 2s. 8d. and the rear cabin 1s. 9d. The journey lasted from 8 a.m. to 4 p.m., at a speed of 4 mph. A stopping place at Scarisbrick opened up a route, by cart, to Southport.

The canal has also made Halsall a favourite spot for anglers. Carp, bream, tench, perch and chubb are caught, with eels coming in from the River Douglas.

When the railways stole the passenger trade, the canal was useful for transporting, among other things, manure. The agreement to sell land for the canal stipulated that free transport was available for the estate. One of the great assets of local farmers, says P. J. Gooderson,[9] 'was the ready availability of town "night soil", which was used in large quantities in the Ormskirk area, thanks to the Leeds and Liverpool Canal.' He continues, 'As Lord Derby, later Prime Minister, told the county agricultural society, "where there's muck there's money".' There were 16,000 horses in Liverpool, each producing four tons of droppings a year. 'If properly made up with straw litter,' says F. M. Thompson,[10] this 'was the basis of 12 tons of good manure; but if left about in the streets was just four tons of nuisance.' Bits of pot and other items are still dug up locally in fields where the cheaper variety of manure was used. Although the fertiliser added to the productivity of the area, it must have made Halsall a rather smelly place! A barge carried 45 tons and the cost was 30 shillings a load – hence the name 'Thirty Bob Muck'.

In addition to manure, Liverpool's household rubbish and street sweepings also came through in 40-ton boat loads at 30 shillings a time. The cinders made the land that much heavier and less likely to be blown about in March winds.

The navigators – given a hearty meal in Liverpool on the evening of the opening day – had a reasonably easy job constructing the West Lancashire part of the canal. Halsall was the only place where excavation work of any consequence was required. For some unknown reason, the canal company was unwilling or unable to take advantage of a slight variation in the route which would have avoided the obstacle. To minimise the task, the canal was made narrower at this point than at other parts. Demand necessitated the widening of the cutting in 1844 to accommodate two barges passing – even then the operation was difficult. Until the improvement, approaching bargees had to crack their whips – used to urge on the towpath horses – to signify their approach. The 'first crack of the whip' gained priority for getting through Halsall.

Early roads were obviously no more than tracks. Thomas Eccleston, drainer of Martin Mere, had to transport his 1767 purchase of an iron plough, bought in Scotland, by sea via London and Liverpool. Even by 1844, T. Weld Blundell was complaining to his neighbour Lord Sefton that 'the roads in every direction are execrable'.[11]

'The first major development', says Alistair Much,[12] 'came not with the improvement of roads but with the growth of a canal system'. 'The canals, which carried huge loads of bulky cargoes such as coal and salt as well as packet boats with passengers, were of enormous importance in the economic development of the North West', says David Stenhouse.[13]

With the advent of railways, Halsall was caught up in the Southport Railway boom. A petition to the House of Lords in June 1847 complained about the 'advantages possessed by watering places which enjoy such ready means of access with large towns have been strikingly exemplified, to the great injury of Southport, in the instances of the neighbouring towns of Lytham and Blackpool, which as watering places are much inferior to Southport in size and importance'.[14]

This sense that Sandgrounders were second class citizens began to be put right a year later with the opening of 'The Shrimp Line' along the coast from Liverpool to Southport. This was only two months before the death of the Manchester–Liverpool Railway pioneer George Stephenson and, from then on, railways aplenty were built in the area (exemplifying the great Victorian/Edwardian fear of monopoly!). The Southport–Wigan Line – later extended to Manchester – was ready in 1855. The link with Preston (the West Lancashire Railway) was begun in 1873 and was ready in time for the 1882 Preston Guild celebrations. Two year later, we had the Southport and Cheshire Lines Extension Railway. Known as 'The Never Never Railway', because it never realised the claims made for it, the line came out of Manchester Central via Aintree, from whence it went to either Liverpool or Southport.

Halsall got in on the act through the Liverpool, Southport and Preston Junction Railway opened in 1887. With stations at Halsall and Shirdley Hill, the 7-mile-long line linked the Cheshire Lines with the Southport–Preston (West Lancashire Railway) line. The idea, never achieved, was to by-pass Southport and have direct trains from Liverpool to Preston. Coming off the Aintree to Southport Cheshire Lines stretch at Hillhouse Junction, the Junction Railway went through Barton (later called Downholland), Halsall, Shirdley Hill, Kew Gardens and Meols Cop, after which it joined the Southport–Preston line.

The 1887 timetable shows 12 trains a day with five on a Sunday. Conventional steam trains were used but, from 1906, a distinctive steam

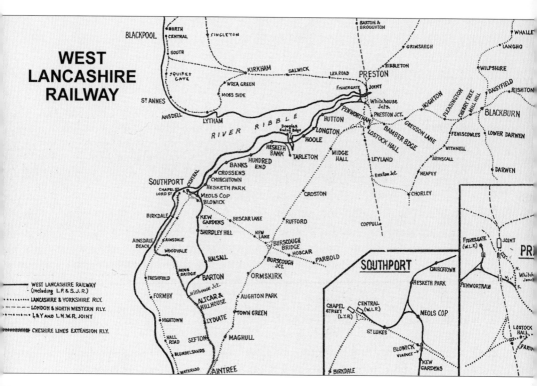

car nicknamed 'The Altcar Bob' (to some 'The Coffee Pot') made its appearance.[15] Operating originally out of the Southport Derby Road Station of the West Lancashire Railway, The Altcar Bob came through St Lukes, Meols Cop, Butts Lane Halt, Kew Gardens, Heathy lane, Shirdley Hill, New Cut Lane, Halsall, Plex Moss Lane, Barton and Altcar at the end of the journey, the car simply reversed like a tramcar with the driver at controls on the coach end and the fireman stoking at the steam end. Guards working the line included Jimmy Drake and Harry Lumley.

In 1897, both the LS & PJR and the West Lancashire Railway fell into the hands of the Lancashire & Yorkshire Railway – the very giant they had been set up to challenge! The passenger service on this line served by The Altcar Bob came to an end on the 24 September 1938, the Altcar Line having been diverted from Derby Road to Chapel Street in 1901. The startling fact was that only 6 passengers a day were using the trains. Engine Driver H. Marshall (who happened to be a JP) drove the last train – a 'Puffing-Billy' as it happened – and Halsall Station Master Thomas Shaw was pictured by the Southport Visiter shaking hands with him.

A public meeting presided over by James Livesley, Chairman of the Halsall Parish Council, was held in St Cuthbert's Hall.[16] A quarter of a

Two wonderful old photographs of Halsall Station and its staff.

century later, the closing of country lines evoked headlines like 'Oh! Dr. Beeching, what shall we do?', but, in contrast, the 1938 Halsall meeting was very low key. No words of dissension are reported; assurances were given – and presumably accepted – that every effort would be made by the Ribble Bus Company to provide adequate alternative services. The

The staff in this picture include Fred Baxter (second left), the stationmaster; Eric Battersby (left), booking clerk; and porter Tommy Shaw (second right), later to become stationmaster.

Tom Shaw is second from left in this view.

route was altered from Moss Lane to go down Turning Lane and into Southport's Scarisbrick New Road for the special convenience of Shirdley Hill residents. There was even the possibility of three Southport buses a

Shirdley Hill Station (*above*) and the Parish Council's tribute to Stationmaster Shaw (*below*).

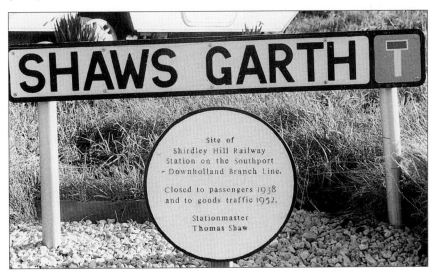

day from Shirdley Hill, and workman's fare, Scarisbrick Arms to Southport, was to be reduced from ten to nine pence!

Rector Mather asked the West Lancashire District Council to give its attention to the road surface in Heathy Lane and the meeting made strong representations for a 30 mph speed limit through the village.

After the final closure, the track was pulled up, with the exception of the section Butts Lane (in the Blowick area) to Shirdley Hill. These became storage sidings, 'giving the strange spectacle', says Cedric Greenwood,[17] 'of continuous lines of coaches and wagons stretching for two and a half miles across the open country'. In more prosperous railways days, the line was useful for the day-time storage of excursion trains which had, earlier in the day, brought the trippers to Southport who needed to return to Manchester or Wigan in the evening.

Rolling stock and track disappeared in 1964, and Southport to Manchester trains, some of which went through Blowick Station (now no more), were re-routed through Meols Cop and, therefore, still used part of the old LS & PJR track.

If the line had held out for one more year, its closure could well have been delayed. Conservation of oil supplies was certainly in the public interest once World War II started, and no doubt it was the war which delayed the final closure for freight traffic until 19 January 1952 – a bad month for local railways. Lord Street Station – the Southport terminus of the 'Never-Never Railway' – closed for passengers on 5 January and the Altcar freight service disappeared almost unnoticed hard on the heels of the Cheshire Lines closure.

Commenting on the latter, 'Traveller' wrote to the *Southport Visiter*.[18] 'The closure should be a timely warning light to railwaymen throughout the land. Unless [he said] they put everything they can into making the railways economically sound, much worse will follow'. Perhaps, if his advice had been followed at the time, Halsall would have been saved from the problems common now to almost every village community – vehicles far too heavy for country roads, insufficient bus services and legions of school buses. It is unfortunate that a village that had the early advantage of pioneering forms of transport should now be no better off – perhaps even worse off – than most other villages.

CHAPTER ELEVEN

The Creation of the Devil

A foolish man who built his house upon the sand. [1]

I F GREAT EMPHASIS is put upon Halsall's association with rock, its near neighbour, Shirdley Hill, is equally associated with sand. Legend has it that the hamlet is a product of the Devil and he is credited with the building of The Devil's Wall – nickname of one of the Clieves Hills near Aughton. The sand for this wall (says the legend) came from the beach and was gathered up in apron-fulls (in his 'brat'!) by the Devil, who flew it to the wall. On one occasion, the story continues, the apron-strings broke and the sand lost en route produced Shirdley Hill!

Nowadays it's a hill that isn't! The name 'Shird' seems to come from the old English 'a clear well', with the suffix 'ley' meaning a clearing. An 1846 map shows the existence of a well in the hamlet. 'There's a slight rise when you arrive', says a *Lancashire Life* writer,[2] 'albeit one hardly sufficient even to make a cyclist pedal harder ... You pass a few farmsteads, bungalows and houses and its, goodbye, Shirdley Hill, almost before you realise you're there'. The suggestion of 'clearing' is perhaps 'a clearing in the marshy ground'.

The 1931 *Gazeteer*[3] sums it all up very briefly: 'Shirdley Hill – place with railway station, LMS SW Lancashire, 3 miles SE of Southport'. At least, as we have seen, there was once a railway station. It was the confident hope of those promoting nineteeenth-century railway lines to Southport that their enterprise would lead to the development of the areas between the main centres of population. This certainly happened in places like Birkdale, Formby, Hightown etc. on the Liverpool–Southport line. But the lack of such development between Preston and Southport and on the Cheshire Lines and the LS & PJ Railway was the reason for their ultimate closure. 'Expansion has been slow', says *Lancashire Life*, 'thanks, presumably, to the rare quality of the encircling fields'.

But in the days of the railway, the Station House was a hive of activity. Thomas Shaw is a well-remembered stationmaster[4] who started life as porter at Barton. He was at Shirdley Hill for the last 30 years of the passenger operations and was then supervisor of freight movements between Kew Gardens and Barton until his 1948 retirement. A parish councillor for 36 years, Thomas was also leader of the Methodist Chapel. Three sons and three daughters were born in Shirdley Hill and one son, at least, succeeded his father as a railway employee. A daughter – Mrs Celia Higson – was booking clerk at the Hillside and Birkdale Stations on the Liverpool–Southport line. Recalling her experiences on the LS & PJR, she spoke of the oil lamps at the request halt which were so dim that a match had to be struck or a torch flashed if would-be passengers wanted the train to stop. The railway level crossing was a little up Renacres Lane towards the former chapel.

It was the goods yard, she said that subsidised the passenger service. Vegetables, straw and hay were carried and manure came into Shirdley Hill. The railway, apparently, was of more local use to farms than had been the canal! 'I always remember the manure wagons', she said. 'The yard was sometimes full of them'. The trade was, no doubt, an extension of that operated by the canal. Closure of the line meant that last postal collections from Shirdley Hill were at 4:30 pm, instead of 6:45 pm. 'If all the railway employees had been as committed as Tom Shaw', says a resident who knew the railway in its heyday, 'the line would never have closed'.

The family moved to 29 Renacres Lane from 1940 onwards and Thomas Shaw died in 1962. It is a tribute to him that the Halsall Parish Council have marked the site of the station with a handsome plaque. It is sited at

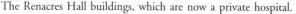

The Renacres Hall buildings, which are now a private hospital.

Renacres Hall.

the corner of Renacres Lane and, significantly, Shaws Garth – a new road with modern bungalows. What an imaginitive title for an area which was once the station yard and station house garden – Shaw after the house's tenant, and 'garth' a Norse word for garden or yard.

Any mention of Shirdley Hill must be accompanied by a brief look at the history of Methodism in the Halsall area. With the dominance of the local Anglican Church, it is not surprising that non-conformity has had a struggle. Sometimes, Halsall Methodists drew large numbers to their small building, but usually they have 'soldiered on with a very small membership',[11] which was decreased in the 1840s by a dispute within the denomination caused by the breakaway of the 'Wesleyan Reformers' (lay folk who revolted against the very strong control of the Methodist Conference over local chapel and circuit affairs. Methodism lost 100,000 members through the dispute).

In 1778, 40 years after Wesley's conversion, there were 10 Halsall Methodists on roll 'and even this number dwindled'. There is no entry in the 1845 Circuit Book but an appearance in 1858 records suggests that there are, at least, some members who have survived 'The Reformers' revolt. That year the first chapel was built in Small Lane North – a tiny wooden building with a very heavy slate roof known affectionately as 'The Match

Box'. A stove in the centre was a welcome luxury at which to warm your feet during Sunday School. Members of the congregation travelled from miles around despite the rival attraction of the Primitive's 'Buttermilk Chapel' at the corner of New Cut and Renacres Lanes in Shirdley Hill. The Halsall Christmas Day Tea Party in aid of Foreign Missions was a particular attraction. But, despite all, a report at the turn of the century [12] describes Halsall as a 'feeble cause'.

When enemy planes were being chased out of Liverpool, they sometimes jettisoned their bombs in the Southport area and on 27 April 1941 one landed in a field behind 'The Match Box'. (The Halsall incident was in the same period as damage to the Birkdale Home for Blind Babies.[13]) The Halsall chapel roof fell in and the building had to be demolished, although the floor was salvaged and sold to the owners of Heaton's Mill in Morris Lane, and some furniture is in the redesigned Rufford Chapel. Happily, St Cuthbert's gave the churchless flock a temporary home, and sometimes they met in each other's houses. A new building was opened after the war in 1950 in Northmoor Lane after nine members had raised £1,000 towards the cost. The building, in Morris Lane, is now imaginitively redesigned as a private house.

The original Shirdley Hill Chapel has been mentioned. Why was it called 'The Buttermilk Chapel' – was it the refreshment available to the congregation or, as sometimes happened, was the chapel in a farmyard? The chapel was part of the Primitive Methodist tradition. James kellett of Mawdesley had preached to a small group in the open air in Knob Hall Lane, Marshside, Southport and from that a group of 'Prim' chapels developed. The 'Halsall Moss' chapel was ultimately associated with the Cemetary Road, Southport, meeting and was established in 1865. When the Primitive Methodist Church held its national conference in Southport in June 1909, Halsall Moss did not figure in the list of chapels for conference preachers on the Sunday, suggesting that perhaps numbers did not justify the sending of anyone from Southport.[14]

But the chapel was replaced in 1925 by the building in Renacres Lane which still exists and has been put to an alternative use. Whereas Halsall Methodists looked to Ormskirk and the Wesleyan Methodist Circuit, Shirdley Hill were of the Primitive Methodist tradition and were part of the Southport Circuit, with Thomas Shaw as chapel leader. There was a Sunday School, which once had 20 pupils, and visitors to the Good Friday Church Anniversary were always assured of generous country hospitality.[15]

The last such event was on Good Friday 1976 and coincided with the last services in the building. Fortunately, a worthwhile alternative use was

The Guides/Brownies have taken over the disused Shirdley Hall Methodist Church.

found for it. With the help of The Prince's Trust and Lancashire County and Sefton Councils, the Sefton Girl Guide Association bought the building in 1975 for £8,000. Two £3,000 projects were undertaken adapting it to provide accommodation for 24 guides/brownies. The grounds have been extended with the purchase for car parking of land to the north of the building, from Brian Webster's Manor House Farm.[16] There is now a layby for coaches and the local council has provided a street lamp – both helping safety in the narrow lane. Opened in on 7 October 1977 by Lady Patience Baden-Powell, wife of the grandson of the founder of the scout movement, the building is well used with guides and brownies coming from as far away as Manchester, East Lancashire and even the Midlands. It is equipped to cater for the handicapped.

Returning for a moment to the 1925 opening of the Methodist Chapel, it seems that the Anglicans were determined not to be outdone. Four years later, 13 October 1929, they opened St Aidan's – a mission church to Halsall. It fared better than St Cuthbert's other mission church at Barton opened three years before Shirdley Hill and burnt down in 1967. Like the nonconformist building in Renacres Lane, St Aidan's no longer functions as a place of worship. It is used now as a village hall.

The Devil may or not have been responsible for a Shirdley Hill sandhill which is now no more – the sand ABOVE the surface – but a sandhill can still be seen in the field across the lane from the Brownies' building! But what makes the hamlet more talked about throughout the whole region – and represents yet another example of how the Halsall area was so uniquely involved in the Industrial Revolution – is the sand UNDER the surface! No satisfactory study of the geology or soil structure of West Lancashire is possible without acknowledging the existence of this sand – Shirdley Hill sand. Experts are divided.[17] Some say that the layer of coarse windblown sand with well-ground grains, which is only a few feet thick and overlays the boulder clay, has arisen because of the original existence of Martin Mere, the lake once to the east of the area. Shirdley Hill would not have been very far from the edge of this badly-disciplined stretch of water. Others claim that there has been a long-term retreat of the sea and that the coastline was once very different from what it is today. The 1977 *Lancashire Life* writer (JB) subscribes to the idea that the West Lancashire coastline was once very different: 'Shirdley Hill was once also where England started, if you happened to be crossing the Irish Sea. But it was about 5,000 BC when Shirdley Hill was part of the cliff known as the Hillhouse coastline. As the sea receded, it left exposed a vast sandy beach: Shirdley Hill Sand'. It seems that this sand is about four feet below the surface in significant parts of the area between The Yarrow, with its Chorley connections, and the Alt, running from Huyton to Hightown. It extends as far inland as the Clieves Hills near Aughton and towards St Helens. 'Hence', says the Lancashire Life writer, 'that town's glass industry, largest in the country' (*The Story of Pilkingtons* (1826–1976) [18] confirms this). 'The Shirdley Hill sand, a deposit ten feet thick which is to be found a little below the surface over a considerable area to the north of present-day St Helens', says T. C. Barker, 'is admirably suited to glassmaking on account of its low iron oxide content. Indeed, it is one of the the very few places in the whole country where such high grade sand and coal occur together'.

Pilkingtons, which began operations in 1820, will now tell you that their sand comes from overseas but it is certainly a fact that the remote hamlet of Shirdley Hill, giving its name to a particular brand of sand, has very close connections with the business which, T. C. Barker said in 1977, provided 'almost all the windows and other forms of flat glass for the buildings of Britain, windscreens for British-made cars and a number of glass products', and was founded on that Shirdley Hill windfall which, thanks to its low iron-content, makes colourless glass.

Shirdley Hill is also well known as the location of Renacres Hall, built in 1640, and named after the moss to the north of the hill. On the road between the hamlet and Halsall and now an exclusive private hospital, it was once a farmhouse working some of the 'rare quality fields' and was known as 'The White House'. Walter Jesson [5] describes a visit there in the autumn of 1953 when Mrs Higson (no connection with the Liverpool Brewery) said that the building once had a beerhouse. There were still rooms with oak beams, one being called 'The Mission Room', suggesting that church services were once part of the routine. It had a raised platform for the speaker but the use, at the time of the visit, was for plucking fowl. Renacres was originally 'Rannickers' – the site, from another description, of a 'little old house where ale was kept', half hidden in trees at the crest of the hill.[6] The last tenants were the Hesketh family and, after their departure, most of the buildings were unused except for two occupants in separate wings. One of these was a market gardener called Jack Higson whose family were very much associated with local agriculture.[7] Gates nearby were once to a driveway now covered over, but there are people who were living in the area in the 1950s who recall coaches with their postillions using the drive.

Like many parts of the Halsall area, Shirdley Hill is remote. In very few cases, can people be said to live 'on top of one another'. The continuing isolation is confirmed by the amazing fact that a gas supply was not available in Shirdley Hill until as recently as 1995. This seclusion was obviously an attraction to builders in the days of Queen Anne of La Mancha in the fields between the hamlet and Renacres Hall. Judging from their choice of name, the area reminded the first owners of either central Maxico or a region of Spain! It is a two-storey house of handmade brick which has listed status and was built in early Victorian times. The stairway is said to have open string and stick balusters and a handrail decorated with wreaths. There are magohony doors and fireplaces with Grecian details.[8]

One-time resident Major Cuthbert Blundell was an enthusiastic competitor in the Waterloo Cup and had large training kennels in the grounds. He never won the cup and must have been envious of another competitor called Pilkington, whose dogs were also trained in these kennels and which, unlike the Blundell dogs, brought home the silver! The Pilkington dogs had names beginning with 'P' – Pentonville, Pincurl and Perambulate while the Blundell dogs had names beginning with 'B'. H. C. Pilkington was a Hoylake stockbroker and his dog Pentonville, trained by Bob Wright, won the 1925 Waterloo Cup. The fullest possible mileage was obtained from the victory, with the dog even making a ceremonial visit to the Liverpool Stock Exchange. He was offered a huge bone and dog biscuits but, said the newspaper report,[9] 'he was apparently not hungry'. In April, Mr Pilkington entertained 60 farmers and gentlemen from the

Halsall district at a local 'do'.[10] He had two other Waterloo Cup victories. But there was some consolation for Major Blundell. He sometimes managed to win trophies from the less prestigious South Lancashire Coursing Event run on his local land. In later years the house was the home of Hilda Blundell – much respected in Halsall – who married Major Lethbridge.

The impressive La Mancha (*above*) and a not so impressive former lodge!

CHAPTER TWELVE

And What More Shall I Say?[1]

His sayings are generally like women's letters; all the pith is in the postscript.[2]

M OST OF THE MATERIAL gathered for a survey of this sort fits well into certain categories covered in appropriate chapters. But, inevitably, there are significant numbers of facts that do not readily blend into the main text – what accountants call 'sundry items'. This chapter seeks to provide a home for these miscellanea.

Local place names

Even a cursory glance at the local map indicates that Halsall has some interesting names for its areas, houses, farms etc. Some are quite colourful. Green Kettle House is on Plumpton Lane off Carr Moss Lane and there is Trundle Pie Lane. How did these names come about? 'Trundle' means 'to move heavily on',[3] and certainly the original state of the roads would justify such a title, but where the kettle and the pie come in is a mystery! There are many places obviously named after the people with which they are associated – Gregory Lane, Bristow Farm, Morris Lane, Watson House etc. Some names suggest the location of various facilities – Mill House Farm and Malt House Farm. Plumpton – as in Plumpton Lane – appears elsewhere in Lancashire and means 'a plum tree';[4] The Runnel opposite the church gets its name from a sixteenth-century word meaning 'a small stream'.[5] Could 'plex' in Plex Lane have a Latin origin and refer to 'an intricate network or arrangement'?[6] There is certainly this sort of network of lanes over the moss!

Carr Moss Lane must have got its name in the fifteenth century, the Old Norse word 'carr' meaning 'an area of bog or fen in which scrub, especially willow, has become established'.[7] 'The Sniddle' was off Carr Moss Lane – the word apparently meaning 'dead grass on a pasture in places that have not been properly grazed'. The Old Mare's Lane – now Mere Lane – went from the main road to the canal at Halsall Hill. The track down by the school was called 'Alikers'.[8] Four Lane Ends, where Gregory Lane joins the main road, is called 'The Owlers' – a local dialect name for the alder tree, which was once a feature of this corner. There are still trees there but, sadly, no alders!

Shirdley Hill's Turbary Farm is certainly a reminder that there was a legal right to cut peat for fuel. Sylvia Harrop[9] tells us that the Halsalls owned 1,000 acres of land providing turves which could be dried and used as fuel. Taking Nicholas Blundell's diary[10] as a guide, she points out that 'delving for turf began in April and continued throughout the spring and summer, with June and July being particularly busy months'. Special long spades were used and the turf was left in the fields to dry. When dry, the fuel was stored in stacks near the cottages requiring it – a practice 'that can still be seen in the Scottish Highlands and Islands today'. Halsall has also been famous for 'light turf' cut into shies or sticks for use as candles. Wood reputed to burn even under water was also once marketed.

The name of 'Grange' Farm means 'an outlying establishment from the Lord of the Manor's or the monastic establishment'.[11] Could the word 'hey', as in Morris Hey and Marsh Hey Farm, mean a wood or what was once a wood? Certainly, Liverpool's Alder Hey rather suggests this.[12] But Jim Sephton says: 'The word 'hey' was, in my opinion, the dialect word for 'field'. There were names like Big Hey, Little Hey, Mucked Hey ('mucked' meaning 'three-cornered'), Shepcote Hey, Barton Hey and many more.'

There were other names very much of local origin. The Northmoor Lane bridge over the canal was always known as Harry Seargent's Bridge because his farm was near it. It was only during the war, when certain areas had to be officially specified, that the proper name of Holme's Bridge was rediscovered. Mere Lane was similarly generally known as 'Mow Lane'.

Halsall during World War II

Rector Mather was at the Parish Church for the whole of the wartime period and would have had responsibility for services on National Days of Prayer and VE and VJ Thanksgiving services, as well as seeking to keep his flock as heartened as possible during the darker days of the conflict. There were, no doubt, numerous occasions when there were funerals and bereavement-counselling for families who lost husbands, sons and daughters. Having lost a son themselves, the Mathers were in a good position to empathise. The establishment of the new playing field on the main road, bought by public subscription, is a memorial to those who died in the Second World War. There are the names of ten men who died in the war on the list, including Lieutenant Mather of the Cheshire Regiment. The original sports field between the church and Halsall House was ploughed up under the 'Dig for Victory Campaign'. Those in the village at the time remember sprouts being one of the crops. When no longer needed for food production, the land had a spell under the cultivation of the Scarisbrick gardening firm of Vincents who used it after the war to grow bulbs.

Various wartime organisations were set up. The Home Guard started training at Scarisbrick Hall where Sir Everard Scarisbrick was CO and a local HQ was established at Halsall Station. Pill boxes and road blocks lined roads across the moss and on the canal. These were manned every night – one duty night in six – in the early days of the invasion scare. (There was at that time a new fortified line along the canal with a series of fortified pillboxes.) Several bombs and land mines did fall within the parish because when bombers were being chased out of Liverpool during the blitz they were not averse to jettisoning their bombs in the neighbouring area. The most significant incident, as we have already recalled, was on 27 April 1941 when an enemy plane crashed in the area and souvenir hunters were at the scene quicker than the authorities! Villagers were well aware that enemy planes were in the area. Apart from the distinctive drone of German engines, there was the the very close beam of searchlights based on Gerard Farm, Barton, and near the Scarisbrick Morris Dancers. The village also had a depot for the Auxiliary Fire Service, and Air Raid Precaution Wardens, Fire Watchers and a unit of the Air Training Corps were assembled. Overall, though, Halsall's war was not a bad one, with little damage and no casualties.

The school had to share its accommodation with Liverpool evacuees. 'Although war has been declared, school assembled as usual', says the 4 September log book for 1939.[14] 'After inspecting gas masks, and practising putting them on, school was closed in accordance with instructions until a specified date'. It was as though having a gas mask was a protection against air attack in itself! No doubt to the disappointment of the children, the delay only amounted to a week. Use of the school building was in conjunction with St Cuthbert's Hall – the old school. The only Liverpool school mentioned by name is Toxteth Technical School and alternate use was made morning and afternoon of the two sets of buildings. In the absence, during the early years, of serious bombing the evacuees gradually drifted back home.

St Cuthbert's Hall was then taken over by the RAF and there were cables under the school playgound for communication with Woodvale. This tenancy was of short duration. 'A month or two later', says a former resident,[15] 'they packed up and never returned. Some years later, thieves dug up the cables on the moss where it was quiet. They were made of copper and worth something'. Meanwhile, as the war continued, so did village life: 'Prizes distributed by Lady Lethbridge', says the 21 December 1939 school log book entry.

The section of the main road running from the present Rectory (Gesterfield Farm) and Cross Lane is still known as The Barracks – a suggestion that World War I soldiers and horses were stationed in the area. But 'barracks' is also a word used for accommodation for Irish labourers, brought into the area for the potato harvest, although Scarisbrick Hall did accommodate troops in World War I and was a hospital in the Second World War. Behind Gesterfield Farm there is a hut which was used, it appears, to house Italian POWs working on the land. There are similar huts in Morris Lane at White House Farm. Our own soldiers also came from Formby's Harrington Barracks to help with potato harvesting. 'They didn't come cheap', says a retired farmer. 'We had to pay the army for their services'. Rather like soldiers of the Roman army of occupation, some of the soldiers/farm workers formed liaisons with local lasses which eventually led to matrimony.

The staffing of banks also changed dramatically during the war. What had been very much a man's domain was invaded – and has never since been evacuated – by women! But even their help was not enough to save Halsall's part-time bank. The branch of the District Bank was closed from 2 October 1939 to 13 May 1946.[16]

Halsall and its near neighbours

Even though Ormskirk is the nearest town geographically, communications with it have not been good. Particularly because of the railway, there have always been strong liaisons with Southport. Even if the railway was used to augment the indifferent Ormskirk bus service, it was necessary to go almost into Southport – to Meols Cop – to get an Ormskirk train via the Burscough Loop and Burscough Junction. Back in history, the boot was on the other foot – Southport once looked to Halsall!

In the 16th century Halsall appointed keepers and pinders to round up cattle on 'score days' in Birkdale and Ainsdale, and to impound them in Halsall 'until the owners thereof have agreed with them for the score and pasture of the same' by paying a charge for 'cowgates' or adjustment. There was a reciprocal agreement in 1516 with Formby.[17]

And Halsall's influence went right to the water's edge. In 1662, 81-year-old William Norrys of Ainsdale, bailiff to the first Sir Cuthbert Halsall and then to Robert Blundell, said that 'all the shipwreck that was cast up, as namely butter and sundry other things, were brought to Sir Cuthbert's manor house and there delivered, and, when any masts, planks, or any other such things were cast up, this authorised officer, sold the same by the direction of Sir Cuthbert and delivered him the money'.[18]

Halsall had similar claims on hay. Sylvia Harrop [19] recalls tithes payable to the Rector of Halsall by Birkdale and Ainsdale farmers harvesting hay from the moss. Right down to the 19th century, Birkdale and Ainsdale farmers leasing land in Halsall were required to attend the Manor Court and take their share of duties there. In the 19th century, there were 15 Birkdale and 8 representatives for Ainsdale. The court dealt with offences such as neglecting drainage and failure to fulfill duties expected as part of the tenancy.

By the same token, the growing Southport was very dependent upon supplies from adjoining country districts. Bailey [20] quotes James Whitehead's account of an early Southport open-air market. 'A few farmers carts, hailing from Halsall, Scarisbrick, Crossens and Banks, brought vegetables, fruit, butter and eggs, and the owners spread out their baskets and hampers on the ground'. There is also an adverse report about the state of present-day Southport's Southbank Road. 'A dirty lane ... always frightfully unpleasant by reason of unremoved cow droppings'. Many of the cows were, in fact, from Halsall and were the source of Southport's milk supply. They were driven every day between the thatched cottages of Upper King Street and the small fields from The Yellow House, in the present-day Eastbank Street area, and Halsall Moss.

Halsall past and present

In 1811 there were 781 people living in the the civil parish, compared with 1,298 at the time of the 1991 census.[21] The age distribution in the latter year was as follows:

	Halsall	*West Lancashire*
0–4	4.5%	6.7%
0–15	10.9%	14.6%
16–pensionable age	61.3%	62.4%
pensionable age	23.2%	16.3%

The figures do not come as any surprise. Halsall has a lower proportion of children aged under 15 than the rest of West Lancashire; we are level-pegging on 16 to pensionable age, with a bigger percentage of retired folk than in the area generally. There were even 12 people in the 90+ category!

Details are given about the economic position of residents over 16. (Figures in brackets represent the percentage in West Lancashire as a whole):

Employees full-time	31%	
part-time	10%	(46.8%)
Self Employed	14%	(7.9%)
Unemployed	3%	(5.5%)
Retired	21%	(17.1%)

Taking a sample of 10% of those employed, the 1991 census gave the following distribution of occupations among Halsall folk:

Managers, administrators, professions and associate professional and technical occupations	33%
Clerical/secretarial	11%
Craft and related occupations	12%
Personal and protective service occupations	16%
Sales occupations	7%

A similar 10% was taken to establish the industries in which employees and self-employed were involved. Two figures are worth examination – the first because it is, perhaps, lower than we would expect, and the other because it seems rather high. The figures are:

Sadly there is no longer a Halsall W.I. David Silcock is driving the tractor.

Agriculture, forestry and fishing	7.4%	(5%)
Distribution/catering	31.9%	(17.3%)

There were 784 households (compared to 115 in 1821), and the household sizes are also interesting:

Pensioner living alone	16.9%	(12.9%)
Non-pensioner living alone	8.4%	(9%)
One adult with one child	3%	(5%)

Not surprisingly, Halsall had a larger percentage of pensioners living alone and there were fewer one-parent families than in West Lancashire generally, and the average household size in Halsall was 2.42.

The total of 793 households with 771 in permanent accommodation suggests the presence of a few static caravans. 85% of the Halsall houses were owner-occupied (72% in West Lancashire) and 48% (6.2%) were on rental from the local council, compared with 22.3% in the area as a whole. A number of the Summerwood and Linacre Lane council-built properties have been bought under 'The Right to Buy' scheme.

Car availability was also established:

Household(s) in Halsall with	no car(s)	18%
	one	44%
	two	29%
	three	8%

At the time Halsall residents had, between them, a total of 1,017 cars on the road. The figure of 18% of families in Halsall without a car compares with 27.1% in West Lancashire as a whole.

In present-day Halsall, some sheep are reared and, in addition to agriculture there are a number of small businessmen, tradesmen, and produce-merchants providing services for a fairly wide area. Some are linked to agriculture and the motor trade is well represented. There is, as we have seen, a significant number retired folk in the village, as well as professional people who commute into larger centres.

Leisure in the village

Cars have made it possible to travel wider afield for leisure activities, although television keeps people at home in the evenings. A Rose Queen Festival, introduced in the late 1920s grew to gigantic proportions. Silcock's Fair regularly did a spell on the old sports ground and in, the days of the Blundells, there were garden parties and Sunday School activities.

St Cuthbert's Hall is remembered as the centre, in the past, of many

Halsall, 1928–29, won the Colonel White Cup at Haig Avenue.

The team from 1936–37.

Robin Neal, Tommy Threlfall and Johnny Rimmer are pictured in Halsall Juniors FC.

The Halsall FC football team in 1920.

A Halsall team at Haig Avenue, Southport.

Halsall cricket team, 1952.

activities. There were performances by the local dramatic society, and the hall provided billiard and, later, snooker facilities. Badminton was also played and it was a place where football teams could change. Harvest Homes were held and there was a 100-strong bible class for those who had left school with occasional socials organised for class members. The Conservatives rented the hall for whist drives and dances, and Nurse Bond organised similar activities.

But, although many of these are things of the past, like most villages, Halsall still has a good range of local organisations. Beavers, Cubs and Scouts, Guides and Brownies work in conjunction with the neighbouring Scarisbrick parish. Currently, there is no youth club but a Young Farmers' Club meets in St Aidan's Hall in Shirdley Hill. Even though they contributed to the Lancashire Village Book in 1990,[22] there is no longer a Womens' Institute in Halsall. The newly developed parish centre in the school will, hopefully, soon be used for a parish fellowship. The church already has its Summer Barbecues, Strawberry Fayres, Harvest Suppers and Christmas Bazaars. Further education classes take place in the school which also hosts a badminton club. A White Heather Club meets weekly and The Sunshine Club for Senior Citizens is involved in fund-raising, with a Christmas Dinner and Summer Outings. The Sports Club provides cricket, football and snooker.[23] Football has traditionally had a place in the Southport and District League. A 'Memories of Bygone Times' report in the

Halsall is traditionally an Oddfellows' stronghold.

Publicity material for the Oddfellows, Halsall.

A Dart Club Dinner at the Scarisbrick Arms, 1950s.

Southport Visiter (22 September 2000), recalls that Halsall Football Club was formed in 1919 and became members of the Southport League. The team won the Colonel White Cup in the 1928–29 season and The Victory Cup in 1931–32. Four seasons later, they carried off the Senior Charity Cup. A number of players, says the report, went into the professional game – J. Pears, who joined Sheffield United, is cited as an example. Cricket, on the other hand, only came into its own with the opening of the new playing field after the Second War.

Like the rest of West Lancashire, Halsall has traditionally been an Oddfellows stronghold, and a lodge still meets in a private house. The 1917 official handbook for the Manchester Oddfellows area advertises the Loyal Victoria Lodge, established in 1891 and meeting at the Saracen's Head. That it had 180 members with an average age of 34 suggests that the movement had a good following. 'Parents cannot do better than enter their children in the Juvenile Branch', says the publicity. 'Admission Free – Also a Female Branch.'

This particular year book gives a profile of Harry Alty Knowles, who was born in 1856 and worked for 30 years as a wheelwright before becoming

The Rose Queen Ceremony has always been an important event in the village. Both of these photographs date from 1953. In the lower picture comedian Norman Evans crowns the Queen.

Bailiff at Bangor's Green Farm, of which he was also tenant. He had married Elizabeth Sumner of Bangor's Green Farm and was a founder member of the Loyal Victoria Lodge. The couple had three sons who were the first members of the Halsall Juvenile Branch. 'The Lodge', says the year book, 'has become a prosperous branch of the District, and our brother

has rendered the cause devoted services, having passed through the various offices with credit to himself and satisfaction to the brethren'.[24]

The school PTA is also very active. A £5,000+ bonfire night firework display attracts a large crowd and the Rose Queen Festival which includes the erection of a large marquee extends over 2 to 3 days. The first Rose Queen was crowned in 1929, when Peggy Ainscough (later Mrs Whalley) was chosen. The gold watch she received from Lady Johnson of Johnsons the Cleaners has been a treasured possession of hers ever since.

The Parish Council organises a Best Garden Competition. A church millenium project envisages a scheme for the floodlighting of the building. The church building, which is well maintained, is regularly open for guided tours.

A village that was once very much surrounded by water and relied on the rock on which it stood to preserve it, Halsall is now served by well-disciplined and carefully supervised water courses. Mill Brook goes under New Street near the former pub and the church. This represents a watershed, with some of the water going via Martin Mere into the Ribble at Crossens and other water draining into the River Alt. Various water

Tom Webster leads the Rose Queen Parade.

courses may well have been diverted over the years, but, at present, going south-east, the brook then divides. The short brook going south has (as we have seen) the colourful name of Trundle Pie; the brook going east is Aughton Cliffs Brook which ultimately goes on to Aughton Hall. To the west, Mill Brook becomes Plex Moss Waterway, then Barton Brook and

There was once ice-skating on the stream alongside the Scarisbrick Arms.

then Downholland Brook, running near the sewage works near the Alt Bridge and Tescos at Formby.

But gone are the days when Mill Brook alongside what was The Scarisbrick Arms froze in pre-World War II days to make an exciting venue for local skaters. 'We don't get the winters now', said Joe Pimblott in 1979,[25] 'I remember', he said, ' when it froze solid for thirteen weeks, day and night. It started in November and went on right through Christmas'.

Local older former residents have since disputed what the newspaper reported in that 1979 piece. Those quoted were said to be far too young to have known skating on Halsall Dam! It is not felt that there was any local skating after 1908. But what does seem to be beyond dispute is that Jack Buck was the fastest man on ice 'if he had a straight track'. 'Copper', because of his hair, was in a similar category.

The disappearance of such activities is symbolic of the very real fact that Halsall, although it still maintains many aspects of its old world charm, is, in so many ways, very different from the village and parish as some still remember it.

Epilogue

A good play needs no epilogue. [1]

S HAKESPEARE'S PLAYS might not have needed a last word but I am
like the amateur carpenter who has to give the nail that extra hammer
blow the professional knows is not necessary!

The Reverend John Clay, a famous nineteeenth-century chaplain of
Preston Prison, began a lecture about the River Ribble in 1845 [2] by saying
that, with hindsight, he had accepted the invitation to speak 'somewhat
too boldly', and that the subject was one 'to which he should be able to
do but scanty justice.' It is a similar experience for me as I have done the
research for and talked to people about Halsall. So much material is available
from a variety of sources and there will be many omissions in what I have
written; maybe some gross errors! I apologise for these.

But here, on the doorstep of where I have lived for sixty years, is

» an area which helps to demonstrate the contribution made by the
   monasteries to the agricultural development of our countryside;

» land remaining in the same ownership for generations which allows
   us to makes a fascinating study of the traditional squire/tenant relation-
   ships which are so much part of our history;

» an asset which resulted in a real life Hyde Park Duel;

» an estate on which a church has existed since Norman times;

» a place which pioneered education in the area;

» a village which gives us, in its history, a picture, in miniature, of the
   many changes over the century in the Church of England.

And an area which made a unique contribution to the Industrial Revolution
through

» the development of one of the country's most important canals;

» the early development of railways;

» the provision of the raw material for one of the country's most important industries.

Despite all these contributions it is only in recent years that, to my shame, I have really become aware of these and many other aspects of Halsall; a village through which I had previously driven so many times without even a second glance!

The verse from Psalm 16 3 I remember from my days as a choirboy has yet again been confirmed: 'The boundary lines have fallen for me in pleasant places; surely I have a delightful inheritance.'

I hope my presentation of the material will help my readers come to the same conclusion as the Psalmist. I share the hopes expressed by John Clay at the end of his lecture:

> I shall feel myself happy if I excite in any one of you a spirit of investigation into the matter or even furnish any new ideas to such as have no leisure for enquiry.

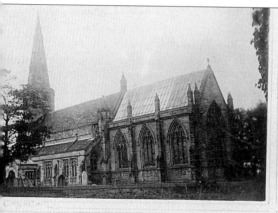

Notes and References

Notes to Chapter 1: A Lovely Village

1. Sign outside an American town.
2. *The Treasures of Lancashire*, North West Civic Trust, 1989.
3. *The Lancashire Village Book*, Lancashire Federation of Women's Institutes, 1990.
4. *A Guide to Halsall and its Church*, W. H. Bullough, 1965.

Notes to Chapter 2: Water, Water Everywhere …

1. *The Ancient Mariner*, Samuel Coleridge Taylor.
2. *Landscape History of West Lancashire*, Dr A. G. Crosby, August 1993 (revised October 1994).
3. *Old Birkdale and Ainsdale*, Sylvia Harrop, Birkdale and Ainsdale Historical Research Society, 1985.
4. *Notes on Southport and District*, Rev. W. T. Bulpit, published by the *Southport Visiter*, 1908.
5. *The Victoria History of the County of Lancaster*, Vol. 3, Farrer and Brownbill, 1907.
6. *Collins Dictionary of the English Language*, 2nd edition, 1979.
7. *Columbia Encyclopedia*, 5th edition 1993, Columbia University Press.
8. *Lancashire in the Nineteenth Century*, John Evans, People's Journal (New Series), Vol. 3.
9. As note 6.
10. *An Introduction to Ancient Churches of the Liverpool Diocese*, Rev. C. W. Budden, Liverpool Diocesan Publishing Co., 1929.
11. Notes on the Parish and Church of Halsall, Taylor and Radcliffe, *Transactions Hist. Soc. Lancs and Cheshire*, XLVIII, 193 (1896).
12. *West Lancashire Local Plan*, Supplementary Planning Guidance, draft for public consultation, 1996.
13. As note 5.
14. As note 12.
15. Mr Jim Sephton now living in Tarleton.
16. As note 3.
17. I am indebted to Cllr Cropper of Scarisbrick for this information.

18. Newsletter, Friends of the Botanic Gardens Museum, July 1999. Article by Bill Cockcroft.
19. *Ormskirk Advertiser*, 15 March 1973.
20. As note 17.

Notes to Chapter 3: God Bless the Squire

1. 'God bless the Squire and his relations, And keep us in our proper stations.'
2. Mrs Alexander, hymn-writer (1823–95).
3. *Victoria History of the County of Lancaster*, Vol. 3, Farrer & Brownbill, 1907 and a paper by Jennifer Lewis: 'Halsall Hall, Lancashire'.
4. *The Aughtons of Aughton*, published by the author Richard Ball-Howard, 1995.
5. Kenyon MSS 1894, Historical Manuscript Commission, 14th Report, appendix 4.
6. *A History of Preston*, David Hunt, Carnegie Publishing, 1992.
7. *Lancashire History Makers*, Gordon Read, EP Publishing, 1975.
8. As note 3.
9. Source unknown.
10. Jim Sephton now living in Tarleton.
11. *Southport Visiter*, 12 February 1921.
12. Lancashire Record Office; *Ormskirk Advertiser*, 9 September 1920.
13. My thanks to Barry Critchley who has a copy of the 1923 sale document.
14. *British Economic and Social History*, CP Hill, Arnold, 1961.
15. My thanks to Mr A. C. R. Brown of Land Agents Smith Gore, Carlisle.

Notes to Chapter 4: Tucked Away in an Unspoilt Corner

1. *The Treasures of Lancashire*, North West Civic Trust, 1989.
2. *An Introduction to the Ancient Churches of the Liverpool Diocese*, Charles W. Budden, Liverpool Diocesan Publishing Company, 1929.
3. *Notes on Southport and District*, Rev. W. T. Bulpit, Visiter Printing Works 1908.
4. *Penguin Book of Saints*, Donald Attwater, Penguin, 1965.
5. *A Short History of the Church*, Canon W. H. Bullough.
6. *John Betjeman's Collected Poems*, John Murray, 1958.
7. *The Black Death*, Philip Ziegler, Readers Union, Collins, 1969.
8. *Romantic Tales of Lancashire*, Joseph Pearce, *Ormskirk Advertiser*, 1931.
9. As note 2.
10. As note 2.
11. *Collins Guide to Parish Churches of England and Wales*, John Betjeman (ed.), Collins, 1980.
12. *English Parish Churches*, Hutton and Cook, Thames and Hudson, 1976.
13. As note 2.

14. *The Buildings of England: North Lancashire*, Nikolaus Pevsner, Penguin, 1969.
15. Edmund Burke (1729–97), *Reflections on the Revolution in France*, 1790.
16. As note 3.
17. As note 11.
18. *Stained Glass in England*, June Osborne, Frederick Muller, 1981.
19. Shakespeare, *Henry VI, Part 2*.
20. *The Victoria History of the County of Lancaster*, Vol. 3, Farrer and Brownbill, 1907.
21. As note 3.
22. *Illustrated London News*, 28 January 1939, 'Page for Collectors, Church Parade', Frank Davies.
23. As note 14.
24. As note 20.
25. *NIV Study Bible*, New International Version, Hodder and Stoughton, 1988.
26. As note 3.
27. *The Real Lancashire*, Kathleen Eyre, Dalesman, 1983.

Notes to Chapter 5: The Cure of Souls

1. Traditional Anglican service for induction of clergy.
2. William Cowper (1731–1800), 'On Receipt of my Mother's Picture'.
3. *The Victoria History of the County of Lancaster* Vol. 3, Farrer and Brownbill 1907. Most of the details of the Halsall clergy are from this source.
4. *Anglicanism*, Stephen Neill, Pelican, 1958.
5. *The Aughtons of Aughton*, Richard Ball Howard, published by the author, 1995.
6. As note 4.
7. *The Age of Reason*, Harold Nicholson, Constable, 1960.
8. As note 4.
9. As note 7.
10. Oliver Goldsmith (1730–1774).
11. Most references to Canon Blundell are from the *Southport Visiter*, 4 November 1905 at the time of his death.
12. Benjamin Disraeli (1804–81), House of Commons, 1865.
13. *Ormskirk Advertiser*, 19 February 1925.
14. Sale document 6 April 1946, provided by Barry Critchley.

Notes to Chapter 6: Desirable Residences

1. Frances Bacon (1521–1626), Essays of 1625, 'Of Buildings'.
2. Baines (Edward) *History of the County Palatine and Duchy of Lancaster*, 1836 (Vol. 4).
3. *Collins Guide to Parish Churches of England and Wales*, edited by John Betjeman, Collins, 1980.

4. *The Victoria History of the County of Lancaster* Vol. 3, Farrer and Brownbill, 1907.

5. *A Social History of Housing 1815–1985,* John Burnett, Routledge, 1985.

6. *Rural Life in S. W. Lancashire 1840–1914,* Centre for N. W. Regional Studies, University of Lancaster, 1988.

7. As note 5.

8. As note 4.

9. List of Buildings of Special Architectural or Historical Interest, Department of the Environment, District of West Lancashire.

10. *Vernacular Buildings of the Lancashire Plain,* Chitty, Coney, Cooper, Lewis, Samuels and Warhurst, North West Archaeological Trust Report, No. 2 1987.

11. *Ormskirk Advertiser,* 15 March 1973.

12. John Bate article in *Ormskirk Advertiser* about the same time.

13. Barry Critchley.

14. This was, presumably, a family member of which Poet William Cowper (1731–1800). William was cousin of Lady Harriet Hesketh of Rufford Old Hall, hence the possible interest of the family in north country matters.

15. *Buildings of England, Lancashire 2 The Rural North,* Nikolaus Pevsner, Penguin, 1969.

16. *Collins Dictionary of the English Language* – 2nd edition, Collins, 1986.

17. As note 10.

18. As note 13.

19. As note 13.

20. As note 14.

21. I am indebted to Mrs A. Riley Deeds, Custodian, Greenalls Group plc, Warrington.

22. *Village Visiter,* 20 May 1998; my thanks to Angela Birchall.

23. *Ormskirk Advertiser,* 26 February 1925.

24. *Ormskirk Advertiser,* 21 May 1925.

25. *Ormskirk Advertiser,* 21 May 1925.

26. *Yesterday's Britain,* Reader's Digest, 1998.

27. *Southport Visiter,* 20 October 1979.

Notes to Chapter 7: The People, Lord, The People

1.   When wilt thou save the people?
                Oh, God of Mercy! when?
                The people, Lord, the people!
                Not thrones and crowns, but men!
                         (Ebenezer Elliot (1781–1849).

2. Abraham Lincoln (1809–1865).

3. Baines (Edward) *History of the County Palatine and Duchy of Lancaster,* 1836 (Vol. 4).

4. *Ormskirk Advertiser*, 24 July 1884.
5. *Ormskirk Advertiser*, 8 December 1881.
6. *Ormskirk Advertiser*, 24 June and 21 August 1879.
7. My thanks to Derek Hammond, Research Archivist, NatWest Group, National Westminster Bank.
8. My thanks to Philip Winterbottom, Archivist, Royal Bank of Scotland, for this information.
9. *Ormskirk Advertiser*, 26 June 1879.
10. *The Lancashire Village Book*, Lancashire Federation of Women's Institutes 1990.
11. I am indebted to former Halsall resident Jim Sephton, now living in Tarleton, for much of this information about local characters.
12. My thanks to Tescos, Southport and Mersey Travel.

Notes to Chapter 8: The Masses Against the Classes

1. Speech by William Gladstone in Liverpool, 28 June 1886.
2. *Lancaster Guardian*, 16 and 23 June, 16 November and 8 December 1894.
3. *Ormskirk Advertiser*, 19 August 1897.
4. *Gladstone*, Roy Jenkins, Macmillan, 1995.
5. As note 1.
6. As note 4.
7. *Labouring Life in the Victorian Countryside*, Pamela Horn, Alan Sutton Publishing, 1987.
8. As note 3.
9. *The Companion to British History*, Charles Arnold Baker, Longcross Press, 1996.
10. The Minute Books for the Parish Meetings and those of Halsall Parish Council now in the Lancashire Record Office, Bow Lane, Preston.
11. Barry Critchley.
12. As note 7.

Notes to Chapter 9: Built and Endowed

1. Plaque to Edward Halsall, Halsall Church.
2. R. A. Butler, Jubilee Lectures, Evans for University of London Institute of Education, 1952, p. 46.
3. Education and Christian Parents, Peter Cousins, Scripture Union, 1969.
4. As above.
5. Baines (Edward) *History of the County Palatine and Duchy of Lancaster*, 1836, Vol. 4 (page 278n.).
6. *Churchtown in the Parish of North Meols*, J. H. Scholes, Botanic Gardens Museum, 1972.
7. As note 5.

8. School Log Books held in the school. My thanks to Headteacher Mrs J. M. Nield and School Secretary Mrs K. Rankin for their help.

9. *Labouring Life in the Victorian Countryside*, Pamela Horn, Alan Sutton Publishing Limited, 1995 (first published 1976).

10. Education Department, County Hall, Preston.

11. *Ormskirk Advertiser*, 13 June 1929.

12. *Southport Visiter* 20 October 1979.

Notes to Chapter 10: The First Crack of the Whip

1. Lewis Mumford (1895–1990), American author and lecturer on social problems.

2. 'Notes on the Parish and Church of Halsall', Taylor and Radcliffe (1897), *Transactions of the Historic Society of Lancashire and Cheshire*, 48 NS 12 for 1896

3. West Lancashire Local Plan, Supplementary Planning Guidance, Draft for Public Consultation, West Lancashire District Council *c.* 1995.

4. *The Victoria History of the County of Lancaster* Vol. 3, Farrer and Brownbill 1907.

5. Ecclesiastical Memoranda as to Halsall, W. F. Irvine, printed privately.

6. Murray's Directory, WS Connell Ltd, 1955.

7. *North Meols and Southport*, Peter Aughton, Carnegie Press, 1988.

8. *A History of Southport*, F. A. Bailey, Angus Downie 1955.

9. *A History of Lancashire*, P. J. Gooderson, B. T. Batsford Ltd, 1980.

10. *Journal of the Royal Agricultural Society of England*, 15, 1877, p. 486.

11. *Rural Life in S. W. Lancashire 1840–1914*, Alistair Mutch, Centre for North-West Regional Studies, University of Lancaster, 1988.

12. As note 11.

13. *The North West*, David Stenhouse, B. T. Batsford Ltd, 1977.

14. As note 7.

15. *Southport Visiter*, articles by Cedric Greenwood, 29 June 1968 and 22 April 1978.

16. *Southport Visiter*, 24 September 1938.

17. As note 15.

18. *Southport Visiter*, 8 January 1952.

Notes to Chapter 11: The Creation of the Devil

1. St Matthew, Chapter 7, verse 26.

2. *Lancashire Life*, May 1977, article by J. B.

3. *The Survey Gazetteer of the British Isles*, J. Bartholomew 1931.

4. *Southport Visiter*, 22 April 1978, article by Cedric Greenwood.

5. *Betwixt Ribbel and Moerse*, Walter Jesson, reprinted 1992 and reviewed by Angela Birchall, *The Star*, 16 September 1992.

6. *These Charming Acres*, Peter Nodin, 1934.
7. Former Resident Jim Sephton now living in Tarleton.
8. List of Buildings of Special Architectural or Historic Interest, West Lancashire, Department of the Environment.
9. *Ormskirk Advertiser*, 26 February 1925.
10. *Ormskirk Advertiser*, 23 April 1925.
11. Emmanuel, *The Story of Methodism in the Ormskirk Area* (1792–1978), S.J.
12. As above.
13. *Southport Visiter*, 29 April 1941.
14. This information is from the Official Programme for the Primitive Methodist Church Annual Conference, Southport 16–26 June 1909, a copy of which is is in the Southport Reference Library.
15. I am grateful to Mrs Goodridge, former Church Secretary at Shirdley Hill.
16. I am grateful to Barbara Ayland who looks after the present-day centre.
17. *Soils of the Preston District of Lancashire*, E. Compton, Harpenden, 1966
18. *The Glassmakers*, T. C. Barker, Weidenfeld & Nicolson, 1977.

Notes to Chapter 12: And What More Can I Say?

1. Epistle to the Hebrews, Chapter 11 verse 32.
2. William Hazlitt (1778–1830), writing about Charles Lamb.
3. *Collins Dictionary*, 2nd edition, Collins, 1986.
4. *The Place Names of Lancashire*, David Mills, B. T. Batsford Ltd, 1976.
5. As note 3.
6. As note 3.
7. As note 3.
8. Jim Sephton now living in Tarleton.
9. *Old Birkdale and Ainsdale*, Sylvia Harrop, The Birkdale and Ainsdale Historical Research Society, 1985.
10. Tyrer, Frank & Bagley (ed.), The Great Journal of Nicholas Blundell of Little Crosby, Lancs. 3 vols, 1702–1728, *Record Society of Lancashire and Cheshire*.
11. As note 3.
12. As note 4.
13. Emmanuel, *The Story of Methodism in the Ormskirk Area 1792–1978*, SJ, copy in Ormskirk Library.
14. School Log Book.
15. As note 8.
16. Mr Derek Hammond, Natwest Group, Research Archivist, National Westminster Bank.
17. *A History of Southport*, F. A. Bailey, Angus Downie, 1955.
18. *Old Birkdale and Ainsdale*, Sylvia Harrop, Birkdale and Ainsdale Historical Society, 1985.
19. As above.

20. As note 17.
21. 1991 Population Census Halsall Ward Profile, West Lancashire District Council 1996.
22. *The Lancashire Village Book*, Lancashire Federaion of Women's Institutes, 1990.
23. I am indebted to Canon Peter Goodrich, Rector of Halsall, for this information.
24. Manchester Unity Oddfellows Official Year Book 1917, printed by the *Ormskirk Advertiser* and made available by Barry Critchley.
25. *Southport Visiter*, 20 October 1979.

Notes to Epilogue

1. Shakespeare, *As You Like It*.
2. There is a copy of this talk in the Harris Library, Preston.
3. Psalm 16, verse 6, New International Version. I knew it originally in the prayer book wording.

List of Subscribers

NB A dash (—) indicates where subscribers requested anonymity.

1 William J. Cropper, Scarisbrick
2 —
3 Mr and Mrs F.J. Bond, Southport
4 —
5 John and Eunice Prescott, Southport
6 Mrs Joan Hawksworth, Southport
7 David J. Marshall, Eccleston
8 David Loines, Halsall
9 Bill Blundell, Halsall
10 John Houghton, Southport
11 Denis Marshall, Scarisbrick
12 Mr and Mrs J. Wright, Shirdley Hill
13 Jane Adams, Halsall
14 Samuel J. Park, Scarisbrick
15 Mrs M.E. O'Brien, Ainsdale
16 Florence Rigby, Banks
17 Mrs M. Kershaw (née Blundell), Burscough
18 George Michael Wickstead, Halsall
19 Mrs June Whitehead, Halsall
20 Mr and Mrs A.R. Thomson, Southport
21 William and Rachel Rankin, Halsall
22 Mr Roger Charles Dutton, Banks
23 Mrs Louise Mary Price, Burscough
24 Mrs Christine Procter, Halsall
25 Mr and Mrs M.A. Hoofe, Halsall
26 Noel Brownlow and Judy Boyce, Halsall
27 —
28 Mrs Joan Prescott, Ormskirk
29 Isobel Woods, Liverpool
30 Michael George Kissack, Downholland
31 David and Sylvia Corfield, Shirdley Hill
32 Philip and Janet Corfield, Dael and Kyle, Shirdley Hill
33 Peggy Finch (née Fazakerley), Burscough
34 Peter Lisle, Southport
35 George and Irene Holmes, Banks
36 Sheila and Charlie Ward, Halsall
37 Sheila Olverson, Halsall
38 William Marshall, Halsall
39 Michael Tomlinson, Halsall

40   George Tomlinson, Halsall
41   Mrs Hilda Halsall, Southport
42   Stephen A. Moon, Halsall
43   Ben Naylor, Aughton
44   Mr J. Woodcock, Aughton
45   I.M. Sumner, Halsall
46   Mr and Mrs C. Molyneux, Halsall
47   James and Eileen Halsall, Lord and Lady of Renacres, Mawdesley
48   Mr E.D. Bignell, Halsall
49   D. de Shannon, Southport
50   Susan Stephenson, Halsall
51   Mr and Mrs E.F. Evans, Halsall
52   Mr Brian Heaton, Halsall
53   Richard Small, Scarisbrick
54   John Marshall, Birkdale
55   Mr and Mrs T. Owen, Halsall
56   Mr and Mrs J. Owen, Downholland
57   Mr and Mrs P. Baker
58   Margaret Edwards, Scarisbrick
59   James Higginbottom, Scarisbrick
60   Barry Serjeant, Scarisbrick
61   Ernest Sherstone, Halsall
62   Lesley Ann Heathcote, Halsall
63   Dorla Halsall Briggs, Southport
64   Mike Tregent, Scarisbrick
65   Betty and Dennis Knowles, Halsall
66   Mr and Mrs R.E. Messenger, Scarisbrick
67   Mr J. Hellier, Halsall
68   T. Robinson, Ormskirk
69   Christopher Murphy, Halsall
70   Mr and Mrs H.M. Boardman, Halsall
71   Joyce and Peter Holcroft, Haskayne
72   David Brazendale, Crosby
73   Martyn Griffiths, Southport
74   Mrs D.R. Craig, Halsall
75   Mr J.P. Wroe, Halsall
76   Paula Ferris, Halsall
77   Beverley Horrock, Halsall
78   Nadine Maddison, Halsall
79   Roy Kenyon, Halsall
80   Edmund Orritt, Halsall
81   Duncan Rothwell, Southport
82   Jane Cameron, Halsall
83   James Ball, Scarisbrick
84   Brian and June Beilensohn, Halsall
85   Mr and Mrs Allan Carr, Halsall
86   Jim Heaton, Halsall
87   Alan and Joyce Mawdsley, Halsall
88   Jean R. Youds, Halsall
89   Mrs C. Damen, Shirdley Hill
90   G.A. Fox, Halsall
91   Mrs Eunice Prescott, Halsall
92   Mr George Abram, Halsall

93   Mr J. Prentice, Halsall
94   Harry and Jean Priestley, Halsall
95   Mr Denis Olverson, Halsall
96   —
97   John Rice, Halsall
98   Mr and Mrs J.H. Marsden, Halsall
99   Mr and Mrs A. Georgeson, Halsall
100 Derek Gilbert, Halsall
101 Mr Graham Stoker, Halsall
102 Sue and Kevin Gilbertson, Halsall
103 Miss Dawn Jones, Halsall
104 J. Sherman, Halsall
105 Mr and Mrs Killen, Halsall
106 Roy and Tricia Johnson, Scarisbrick
107 Graham and Ann Grimshaw, Aughton
108 Mr J. Farley, Ainsdale
109 Harry Blundell, Halsall
110 Mr Harold Jenkinson, Haskayne
111 Mr and Mrs J. Porter, Halsall
112 Anthony Massam, Halsall
113 Jean Hewitt, Haskayne
114 Cynthia Hartley, Halsall
115 Mrs Teresa Leatherbarrow, Halsall
116 Mrs D.M. Hardcastle, St Asaph, N. Wales
117 Michael M. Currie, Halsall
118 Dr Mona Duggan, Haskayne
119 David White, Halsall
120 Linda McCusker, Halsall
121 Mrs M.C. Hankin, Halsall
122 —
123 Mr and Mrs D. Ainscough, Halsall
124 Mrs Carol Weston, Halsall
125 Yule Family, Halsall
126 John Sharp (Postmaster, Shirdley Hill P.O.)
127 Mr Thomas and Mrs Marianne J. Rawsthorne, Halsall
128 Mrs S. Olverson, Halsall
129 Mrs A. Sumner, Halsall
130 Henry Mawdsley, Halsall
131 Mrs E. Smerdon, Halsall
132 Anthony J. Brothwell, Southport
133 Mr and Mrs Alan Mawdsley, Halsall
134 Mrs W. Lewis, Halsall
135 Antony Tyrer, Halsall
136 John J. Ormsby, Scarisbrick
137 —
138 John F.Y. Duffy, Southport
139 Ray Jeffs, Southport
140 Lena Marshall, Halsall
141 Jane Kasper, Barton
142 Doug and Phyllis Palin, Shirdley Hill
143 Mrs Elsie Massam, Halsall
144 Bob Isaac, Halsall
145 Mrs I.M. Graham, Halsall

146 —
147 Mrs Barbara Irving, Halsall
148 Mrs Edna Marshall, Halsall
149 Mr and Mrs J. Whalley, Halsall
150 Mr and Mrs Egan, Halsall
151 Shirley Orme, Halsall
152 Mrs D. Ball, Halsall
153 —
154 Mrs Patricia Frenzel, Southport
155 M. Howard, Halsall
156 Dorothy Ashton, Shirdley Hill
157 Clifford and Myra Kenyon, Haskayne
158 Dick and Nancy Ainscough, Halsall
159 Capt. J.R. Howel, Halsall
160 Roger and Diane Comfort, Halsall
161 Mr Richard Fairclough, Shirdley Hill
162 Mr Brian Halsall, Barton
163 James John Sines, Halsall
164 Marion Austin, Halsall
165 —
166 Mr John Banks, Halsall
167 Richard Threlfall, Southport
168 Mrs B. Ayland, Southport
169 Richard and Jane Adams, Halsall
170 Evelyn Huyton, Halsall
171 —
172 Mrs P. Neale, Halsall
173 Lena Marshall (Mrs), Halsall
174 Geoff Wilkinson of Halsall House, Halsall
175 Mrs Hannah Shacklady, Halsall
176 Wilf and Beryl Sephton, Barton
177 Mr R. Hesketh, Ormskirk
178 Mrs Edna Marshall, Halsall
179 (Mrs) Mildred Oakes, Halsall
180 Mr John J. Smith, Barton
181 Mr Ian Stevenson, Haskayne
182 David W. Stopforth, Halsall
183 John Craven, Haskayne
184 Cathy Faunch (née Halsall), Parbold
185 Mrs A. Johnstone, Lydiate
186 Mr Arthur Blundell, Scarisbrick
187 Miss G. Bond, Halsall
188 —
189 Mrs Janice Ryan, Southport
190 Mrs Brine, Halsall
191 Keith Bond, Burscough
192 Mr T.H. Thompson, Haskayne
193 Mrs Irene Abbott, Halsall
194 Mrs Barbara Berrington, Ormskirk
195 Mrs D. Pilkington, Halsall
196 Barry and Barbara Critchley, Halsall
197 Florrie (née Critchley) Pilling, Barton
198 Gerry Riley, Chairman of Halsall Parish Council

199	Bob Wilby, Southport
200	Mr A.B. Salmon (Local War Evacuee), Southport
201	Mr Christopher D. Kenyon, Halsall
202	A.H. Gilbert, Halsall
203	Tina Bulmer (née Beddows), Southport
204	Peter Arthur Bradshaw, Crewe
205	Alfred Barclay Hicklin, Halsall
206	Albert Burns Salmon, Southport
207	—
208	—
209	Mike Gee, Halsall
210	Shirley Watterson, Halsall
211	Mr Paul James Halsall, Aughton
212	Mrs K. Rankin, Halsall
213	J. Holcroft, Southport
214	M. Holcroft, Southport
215	G. Holcroft, Southport
216	Mr and Mrs Geoffrey H. Wilkinson, Halsall
217	Mr and Mrs P.J. Dodd, Halsall
218	Mrs Ann Green, Halsall
219	Dr and Mrs Jill Cook, Halsall
220	Mr Anthony Marshall, Halsall
221	Mr Philip Marshall, Halsall
222	Margaret Mansbridge, Ainsdale
223	Chris, Flo and Caroline Dennis, Halsall
224	Ann and Jim Critchley, Scarisbrick
225	Joan and Allan Pyrke, Ainsdale
226	Barbara and Mac Carter, Halsall
227	Brian and Cecelia Webster, Halsall
228	Noel Rynhart, Southport
229	J.M.A. Blundell, Scarisbrick
230	Mr and Mrs S. Massam, Halsall
231	Mrs K. Massam, Halsall
232	Mr and Mrs C. Staples, Halsall
233	Allan Huyton, Barton
234	Clifford Huxtable, Halsall
235	Tom Porter, Ormskirk
236	George Henry Porter, Ormskirk
237	Marjorie Porter, Ormskirk
238	Mrs M.R. Chalmers, Birkdale
239	Rachel Johnson and Mark Johnston, Halsall
240	R. Couchman, Lydiate
241	John Sims, Southport
242	Mr and Mrs J. Ball, Halsall
243	S.C. Foat, Halsall
244	Edward Jones, Shirdley Hill
245	Mr D.W. Beaver, Halsall
246	Bernard Malone, Haskayne
247	D.R. and P. Pomfret, Halsall
248	Ve and Malcolm Wright, Southport
249	—
250	Mrs H.M. Brown, Southport
251	Mrs C. Baker, Birkdale

252	—
253	Mr and Mrs Whitty, Halsall
254	—
255	Mr and Mrs F. Schober, Halsall
256	Roy and Joan Webster, Rufford
257	John Edward Wilcock, Southport
258	—
259	R.W. and R.B. Baxter, Burscough
260	Mr Edmund Orritt, Haskayne
261	Mrs Valerie J. Gaskell, Birkdale
262	Colin and Ann Throp, Halsall
263	—
264	Pam Bialeck, Halsall
265	Mr and Mrs Jackson, Ainsdale
266	Ken Hilton, Burscough
267	Eric and Lilian Ogden, Cheadle Hulme
268	Mrs M. Winstanley, Halsall
269	D.A. Huyton, Halsall
270	John W. and Irene Thorley, Halsall
271	Brian Davies, Southport
272	Paul McIntyre, Halsall
273	Mr G. Corness, Southport
274	Mrs J. Hargreaves, Birkdale
275	David Westley, Halsall
276	Denyse Croston, Halsall
277	David and Anne Goldstraw, Scarisbrick
278	Mr and Mrs K. Hutchinson, Halsall
279	Peter Comfort, Ainsdale
280	Mr and Mrs R. Baldwin, Halsall
281	—
282	Mr Hey, Southport
283	Miss E. Turner, Ainsdale
284	Dr R.A. Yorke, Formby
285	—
286	Victoria Olsen-Abbott, Halsall
287	Mrs S. Pedley, Southport
288	Norman Olverson Ltd, Halsall
289	—
290	—
291	Canon Peter Goodrich, Halsall
292	Barry and Barbara Critchley, Halsall
293	Audrey Garlick, Southport
294	Jim Sephton, Tarleton
295	Geoff J. Wright, Southport
296	Mrs Ruth M. Lewis, Birkdale
297	—
298	Linda Pimlott, Halsall
299	Colleen Cain, Lydiate
300	Mr K. Mawdsley, Halsall
301	—
302	Ron and Jeanne Burgess, Halsall
303	Gerald W. Hogg, Tarleton
304	Doug Daykin, Aughton